Gales Every Weekend

Being the crew's account of *Robinetta*'s 2015 season sailing on the West Coast of Scotland from Crinan to Stornoway and then south into the Clyde.

By

Alison and Julian Cable

Gales Every Weekend

© AJ and Family 2018
146 Stortford Hall Park
Bishop's Stortford
Herts,
CM23 5AP
England

All photos © Julian and Alison Cable except where otherwise stated.
Cover photo, passing Dutchman's Cap 15/07/15

Contents

Preface   p5

Getting afloat, Cairnbaan to Tobermory   p7

Cruising the Hebrides   p17
    Tobermory to Mallaig,   p20
    Mallaig to Lochboisdale,   p32
    Lochboisedale to Stornoway   p40

Heading South   p55
    Stornoway to Tarbert   p57
    Tarbert to Holy Loch   p67

Last Sail of the season
    Holy Loch to Fairlie Marine   p80

Year end Totals   p85

List of Places visited   p86

Gales Every Weekend

Preface

This book is a compilation of the Blog posts we made during 2015, relating to sailing on *Robinetta*, a small wooden yacht built in 1937. Last year we changed the "voice" of the blog so Alison was the "I" when we converted it to a book; this year it is Julian's turn to be the teller of the tale.

The crew are not the obvious choice for long distance cruising. We didn't sail until our late thirties. We get on famously but we do bicker. We are clumsy and forgetful. So we try to sail within, or sometimes just beyond, our comfort zone. Neither of us is the "skipper". We sail as equals in the decision making. With only two people aboard we have to be each other's back up and have made sure we are equally competant.

Robinetta is not an obvious boat for long passages. She is short, wide, deep and heavy with a small engine. We have done what we can with the sail plan and she can do 6 knots off the wind but that does not happen to us very often. So we passage plan on 4 knots and motor sail when we have to to keep that speed up.

Neither is she a particularly safe boat. We have no idea about her theoretical stability and her cockpit drains straight into the bilges. She used to be self draining but a previous owner put enough lead in her to lower the free-board so that the drain holes are underwater. We have a radio, carry flares, and a throw line, and wear life jackets when appropriate, but *Robinetta* is not big enough to carry the safety equipment considered necessary nowadays for long distance cruising; we have no life raft, or Danbuoy, or anywhere to mount them. So we are never going to take *Robinetta* sailing across the Atlantic; but she is strong and stiff and can be reefed single-handed from the cockpit.

In some ways she is the ideal boat for coastal passages. Her limitations force us to plan conservatively. We don't go out if bad weather beyond our experience is likely and we don't try to go further than the crew are fit for. Most importantly we never promise ourselves that we will be in a certain place at a certain time.

These limitations are liberating. Without fixed goals, failure is impossible. Of course we do set goals, we just don't mind if we end up doing something else. Often we change plans to suit the capabilities of boat and crew.

The British Isles are a great place to sail or to be stuck in port. This is true even in places you might not think of as tourist destinations.

Alison and Julian Cable

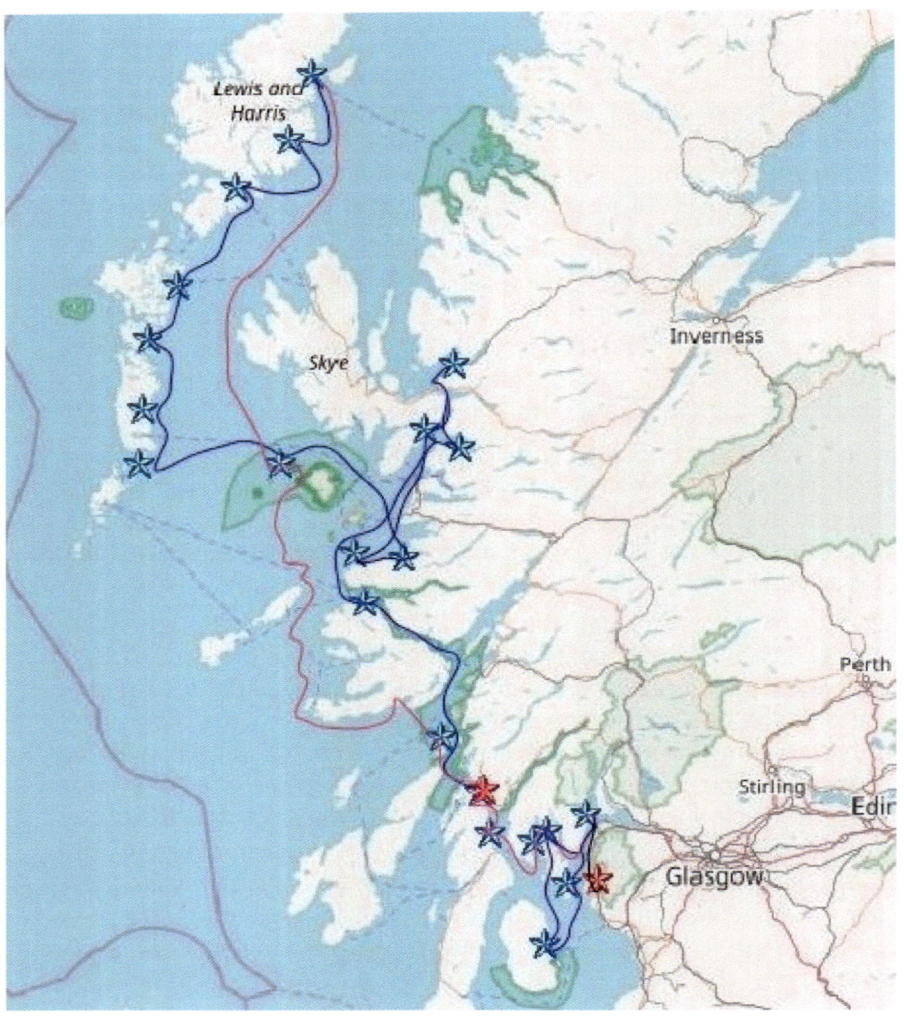

The start point for our year dedicated to the West Coast of Scotland was Cairnbaan, a small settlement on the Crinan Canal, built originally to house the canal workers. We left *Robinetta* ashore there in October 2014, under the care of Adam Way's boatyard. Unfortunately Cairnbaan is a long way from where we live, and we did not get many chances to check up on her.

She did get professionally surveyed at the request of our insurer, and we made sure all recommendations were followed, but otherwise our winter work was less intense that when she was closer to home.

Getting Afloat

Less than a month to the Launch date

29/03/2015

Having *Robinetta* so far away has made winter work an impossibility. Even if it had been possible to take time off work to travel to Cairnbaan we would not have been able to do much. The boat is not undercover, and the days are too short and cold to dry off the dew and let us paint. When *Robinetta* was at West Mersea Alison would sometimes say "Oh, it's dry and warm(ish) today, I'm going to the boat!". She misses that.

Alison, Alex, and I will be heading north straight after Easter, for a week's solid work on her before she goes back in the water in mid April. With lots to do inside as well as out we will be busy whatever the sky throws at us and we are now thinking hard about what we will need to do before we leave home.

The rigging is in pretty good shape, but the hoops that hold the sail luff to the mast could do with some varnish, and some of the serving around the loops at the ends of the wire ropes is worn and needs to be renewed; nothing major, but actually making a start on it after a winter's indolence is hard going.

Adam Way never sent us the quote we asked for about stopping the leaks in the fore-hatch, so we'll have to do something about that, and about the issues highlighted in the new surveyor's report. Alison says she will be spending next week making lists of things that have to be done before *Robinetta* is craned in!

Rushing to get ready

08/04/2015

Alison, Alex, and I got to Cairnbaan at ten this morning, and *Robinetta*'s covers came off to reveal her looking pretty much as she did back when Alison last saw her in November. The surveyor had taken off a little paint to examine the wood, but not so much that it would slow painting down. The bilges were pretty full, but still below the level of the floor boards and the inside did not feel too damp, although the walls are covered with black mould as normal!

The electric pump would not work as the batteries were flat, so I took the batteries out so we could charge them overnight. If they won't take a charge we will have to buy new ones, but they have already outlasted our expectations. They are only cheap caravan batteries and we bought them the first year we owned *Robinetta,* so they owe us nothing.

The weather was bright, dry, and warm; a little too windy for perfection, but excellent for getting on with the outside tasks. All the varnished wood on the foredeck and cabin sides got a coat of varnish, as did the bowsprit and top third of the mast. Alex touched up all the bare wood below the water line, so the hull is nearly ready for a complete layer of tie coat. We just need to get something to fill the holes the surveyor made. There are two chandlers between the cottage we are staying in and Cairnbaan, so we'll buy it in the morning.

Two more days like this, and we'll be happy. Alison says she wants the weather gods to keep smiling!

Alex getting on with the tie coat

Another Great Day

09/04/2015

The weather is holding so far, and outside work is well advanced. We got a complete layer of tie coat on before lunch, and grey metallic primer where it was needed on the topsides, then after lunch it was time for varnish on the mast and bowsprit. The first coat of anti-foul went on mid-afternoon, then the varnish on the foredeck and cabin sides got a second coat.

The essentials below the water-line are done, *Robinetta* could be craned in now, even if the weather broke this evening. There is still plenty of work to do, including checking the through-hulls, before she should really be launched, but the vital, weather dependent stuff is done.

Meanwhile work inside the cabin continued with only one aim, to get rid of the black mould that is growing on all the paint work. We bought some spray on anti-fungal wash from Screwfix, and we all had a go spraying and wiping throughout the day. There is still more of this wonderful task to complete tomorrow...

Neolithic stone carvings at Cairbaan

In between all this work we had a drink on the terrace at the Cairnbaan Hotel, and walked up the hill to show Alex the neolithic stone carvings. We ate our lunchtime sandwiches there, admiring the view down towards the canal. There are better places to keep a boat over winter, and get it prepared for launch, but on a warm sunny April day it's difficult to think of one.

Work goes on

10/04/2015

We did not get much done today compared to yesterday. But that was mostly because the weather changed for the worse and we had to take the afternoon off.

Although we got another layer of varnish on the top of the mast and the bowsprit, the varnish on *Robinetta* herself was still tacky in the morning, and certainly not ready for another coat by the time we left the yard, when it was beginning to spit with rain.

Alex finished the anti fouling, and patched the above waterline paint where it needed it. Unfortunately the new tin of Lauderdale Blue looks a lot darker than the old, and the patches stand out. Knowing that the fresh paint will soon fade to the same shade as the old did not help at this point! (*The next day Alex stirred the paint better, and repainted. The hull is now all one colour!*)

I checked the through-hulls and fettled them. They did not need a lot of work, but we don't want them getting back in the state they were at the beginning of last year!

The inside of the hull is now as mould free as an old wooden boat ever gets, so it's time to get things out of the car and into the boat! I fitted the new radio, but we can't check it out until we have the batteries back in *Robinetta*. One of them seems to be coming back from the dead, but it won't fully charge and we are investigating replacing both.

Adam Way, who runs the boat yard, helped free *Robinetta*'s mast from its cramped and inaccessible storage rack, so I spent the evening looking over the rigging, renewing the serving where it needed it to be ready to start dressing the mast tomorrow.

On Wednesday Alison said she would be happy if we got three good days in a row. We have, and we are feeling really good about our progress! Three people working on one small boat can do a lot in two and a half days!

Afloat!

14/04/2015

We are afloat at Cairnbaan!

We spent the last few days continuing to get *Robinetta* ready, except for Sunday when we drove over to Kirkcaldy to see Alison's parents and collect the cushions we had left there over the winter. Alex stayed there overnight, then got a train home as he did not want to come sailing.

Robinetta was craned into the canal this morning and the mast dropped in around noon. It was a horrid soaking wet day. As we untangled the rigging I realised I had managed to get three separate ropes the wrong side of the VHF antenna cable. The only untangled halyard suitable for hauling someone up to fix it was the one we call "spare" which has no purchase. Luckily the yard people were there to help haul. As usual Alison went up to do the necessary. I've lost a lot of weight but she is still much easier to pull up the mast.

The next problem was with the batteries. As expected they didn't start the engine so we drove up to the chandlers at Crinan and bought one. So we now have one good battery. The remaining old one will start the engine a few minutes after a charge from the engine, but not reliably. We will make do with one until we can get another, cheaper one.

We took *Worm* with us to Crinan on the roof of the car. The staff at Crinan basin were happy for us to leave her beside their office overnight, and coming through the locks will be easier without a dinghy in tow.

Cairnbaan to Crinan

15/4/2015

This morning we bent the mainsail on and headed through the locks with two other boats. One was single handing and had booked an assisted passage so we had the benefit of Scottish Canals staff to take our lines and work the gates and sluices. I helped with the gates.

Lunch stop between the Danardry locks

The canal has now formalised the working day, so that the assisted passage had to pause at lunchtime. We were given the choice of staying in the lock, or leaving it to tie up just downstream. The rest of the group stayed in the lock, but it was too noisy for us with water thundering over the top of the lock gate like a weir, so we took our lines back on board and went on a little further to tie up at a rather pleasant pontoon for lunch.

We got to Crinan about 3 pm, which meant we had missed the north going tide through the Dorus Mor. So we are staying the night in the basin.

We used the time to fill the water tanks and get the new echo sounder working.

Gales Every Weekend

Sailing North?

16/04/2015

Weather reports are essential when planning a day's sailing, so we turned on our brand new radio to get the 22:10 weather update last night. The problem was, we could not hear anything! We called up the coast guard for a radio check, nothing! So now we needed to work out why.

Our brand new DSC radio has never been used before. We now tried it with both the newly connected antenna at the top of the mast and with the spare radio antenna we keep inside the cabin. The old radio had been left in the car at Cairnbaan. The first question we asked ourselves was why neither of us had thought to do a radio check at Cairnbaan! We didn't have an answer to that one!

Robinetta in the Crinan Basin

Refitting the old radio seemed the best idea, but it was in the car four miles away, and it was almost certain that its power lead had made its way into the bin by accident.

I got up early and walked back to Cairnbaan along the tow path, which since it was a bright (but chilly) morning along a scenic bit of countryside was not a hardship. I drove back, bringing the radio with me. The missing power lead did not turn up, but the manager at Crinan boatyard found an

Gales Every Weekend

old spare for a nominal fee. He also told us that the Crinan basin was a well known radio hole, and offered to do us a radio check on his hand held. It worked. The new radio picked his call up on both antennas.

Panic over. We retrieved *Worm* from behind the lock master's office and locked out of the Crinan basin at 0930 into a flat sea, with bright sun overhead, and no wind. We did bend on the No 1 jib and raise the main mid morning, but there was not enough wind to sail, and we soon took them down.

More wind would have been welcome, but being out on the water again, in bright sunshine felt wonderful. We carried the tide nearly all the way north, taking full advantage of the favourable flow through the Dorus Mor and the Sound of Luing, and by 18:00 we were moored up at Tobermory, having motored all the way. Not a bad first day of the season at all.

Approaching Tobermory pontoon   Photo© Sue and Stu from Esseness

Perfect Day Sail

17/04/2015

Ardnamurchan point from the south

Tobermory in April can mean cold nights. We slept wearing woolly hats. But the sunshine was glorious in the morning, and I did some work on the rigging with nothing on top of my tee shirt.

After that we went sailing, or at least motoring in still air to have a look at Ardnamurchan Point with the thought that we would then head for Muck. We saw some thing that was probably a pod of whales in the distance, heading into the Sound of Mull. We were too far away to see much, but they looked bigger than dolphins.

As we got close to Ardnamurchan a breeze sprang up, so we raised the sails. The forecast had promised some wind, 3-4 from the East or North East, and as it came in and strengthened nicely we decided not to beat towards Muck, and instead turned onto a broad reach for Coll. Much better! A seal popped up to have a look at us, but was really more interested in the sea weed it was holding.

There were quite a lot of guillemots about, and a couple of cormorants fishing, plus some gulls too distant to identify. Plenty of birds really, but not a hint of a sea eagle.

Gales Every Weekend

Ardnamuchan light house

At Coll we gybed round and reached back towards the sound of Mull, romping along at 4-5 knots, and touching 6 for a moment. This sort of day is what sailing is about, a good breeze, hardly any swell, and wonderful scenery; the sort that photographs are too small to convey!

The wind disappeared as we got back into the shelter of Ardnamurchan point, and we motored into Tobermory and picked up the buoy where *Robinetta* is going to spend the next five weeks while Alison and I go back to work.

Planning Ahead

When we had *Robinetta* surveyed at Cairnbaan one of the things that the report highlighted was the need to store her undercover over the winter in Scotland. It is not something we thought about doing further south, but it makes sense when we have to plan our visits and can't pick the weather we will have when we get there. Undercover storage is at a premium, and needs booking early, so Alison started looking once we were back from Tobermory.

We were thinking of taking *Robinetta* to the Tarbert Traditional Boat festival, which meant she would be in the Clyde, so she talked to the people at Silvers at Rosneath in the Gare Loch, and to Fairlie Marine. *Robinetta* spent the winter of 1937/1938 at Silvers and they had room, but Fairlie was cheaper, and a lot easier to get to by public transport. It seems we are not that sentimental and we picked Fairlie. We know *Robinetta* has been there too. The designer and first owner Denys Rayner sailed her there from Liverpool with two friends in 1937 and left her on a mooring buoy at Fairlie from the 18th to the 29th of May. He then had a fine cruise, firstly with his wife Elisabeth and then with his father.

Cruising the Hebrides

A complicated journey

23/05/15

After five weeks at home working we are finally heading back north. We had return train tickets from London to Glasgow and single train and ferry tickets from Glasgow to Mull. When we got to Euston we discovered that the line was closed from Carlisle to Glasgow with a rail replacement bus. The bus was great – a fast comfortable coach on the motorway with no stops. With a free shuttle between Glasgow Central and Queen Street it was a trouble free ride. We had an hour or so to wait at Queen Street and headed for a Weatherspoons Pub where we shared a table with a young man who was planning a visit to the Western Isles with his girl friend. We had a nice chat.

At Oban the ferry was delayed because it was waiting on Mull for passengers from a broken down bus. I took the opportunity to head into town and get haggis and chips. Now we knew we were really back in Scotland! We phoned the taxi we had booked to get from the ferry to Tobermory and he was happy to wait. In the end everything was easy, but there were a lot of steps – walk, train, underground train, train, bus, bus, train, ferry, taxi, – before we reached Tobermory. Then we needed to empty the water out of *Worm*, and row across to *Robinetta* in the rainy darkness.

A morning spent on maintenance

24/05/15

Robinetta seemed in quite good condition when we got aboard last night. Not too much mould inside, and not too much water in the bilges. Even better, this morning the engine started first time on the new battery. There have been casualties during the last 5 weeks. *Worm's* port front quarter-knee has come unglued. The string securing the solar panel to the cover broke and the panel was in the water. It doesn't work properly any more. We lost a shackle pin from the bob-stay tensioning gear.

We motored to the pontoon and brought her in beautifully, if I do say so. It made getting provisions aboard easy.

I had ordered a new battery so we would have two new ones. It was safe in the Harbour Office. We got it on board and just for fun tried starting the engine on the old one. It started first time! I decided to leave it in place and keep the new one for when we need it. Without a solar panel a spare is very comforting.

The port battery compartment was in good condition but the starboard one needed some work. In Cairnbaan the nut and bolt for the positive terminal and the metal strap holding the battery in place were both so corroded that I had had to saw then off. So the new battery we bought at Crinan was not tied down and the positive terminal was tightened with a machine screw. The Tobermory chandler stocks battery cable terminals so we bought one and I fitted it. Problem one solved. We took the battery out and the remains of the old strap was held on at the front with a captive machine screw and a nut. At the back a baton screwed to the floor of the locker held the strap. Amazingly the three screws (good bronze ones) came out easily and I was able to cut the nylon strap and fit it as a direct replacement. With everything back in place the strap could be tightened easily and holds the battery perfectly.

The bob-stay was a bit of a problem. It is mainly chain, and shackles to a becket on an old block which has two beckets. The second of these is really thin and we tie a line to that which goes through a double block to tension the bob-stay. It was the shackle connecting the chain to the becket which had lost its pin. The shackle was too big to pass through the becket - it must have been fitted with the block disassembled. We looked in the chandlers for a new block but they had nothing suitable so I bought an undersized shackle that would fit through the becket and sawed off the old shackle. We bought a junior hacksaw handle in the iron mongers. It came with a blade that lasted under a minute. The blades we had bought in Ardfern were made of sterner stuff! One of those made quick work of the shackle and we had a working bob-stay again with the new pin firmly moused in place! We should go over all the other shackles on the boat and mouse them.

That left the damage to *Worm*. Every time I thought about trying to fix the quarter knee back on the rain got heavier. The quarter knees are made white beam wood from our garden. It is lovely wood but it doesn't take glue well and we have no clamps on board.

An afternoon holiday walk with waterfalls

Waterfall in Aros Park, Tobermory

After working hard all morning we could have set off north, but neither of us really felt like it! We had explored the town thoroughly when we were here last year, but this time we had remembered to bring our hiking boots, so we headed off along the shore path to visit the waterfalls. There had been a lot of rain the day before, and the waterfalls were in spate. I brought along my new Finepix S1 camera, while Alison had the waterproof Olympus Tough. We both got some good video and photos.

Tobermory to Isle Ornsay

25/05/2015

After yesterday's preparation day we got an early start from Tobermory. The forecast was not encouraging "Ardnamurchan point to Cape Wrath, W or NW 4 or 5 increasing 6 at times. Sea state rough to moderate". The Minch forecast was almost identical. We wanted to go to Canna today, with the idea of crossing to the Outer Hebrides tomorrow and into Lochboisdale on South Uist. The forecast made that doubtful, but when we left Tobermory at 07:40 it was still possible, so long as the wind was more west, with no north in it.

I bent on the no 2 jib as we cleared the harbour, then took the helm while Alison went below to make porridge for breakfast. We motored up to Ardnamurchan point in calm seas, but with a headwind that made sailing where we wanted to go impossible. None the less we got the reefed main sail up a couple of miles short of the point, where we still had good shelter from the seas. We could have sailed from this point on, but would have been heading for Tiree! We were hungry again so I went below to make a second breakfast of fried egg rolls.

Passing Ardnamuchan Point in the swell

Once we rounded Ardnamurchan we could sail up towards the Sound of Sleat, leaving Muck and Eigg on our port side, so we unrolled the jib and motor sailed on a fine reach, trying to make the course of 28T that I had set toward the Sound of Sleat. After a while Alison realised that we were heading really close to Eigg, so freed off the wind a little. The engine went off at 10:50, and we made a steady 3 ½ – 4 ½ knots, heading past Muck, then Eigg. The seas were not bad, but we were well heeled so Alison had to hold the kettle on the (ungimbaled) stove to keep it there when she went below to make tea. Unfortunately the alcohol in the stove was low, to the kettle took 20 minutes to boil!

We tacked towards Eigg for about ten minutes. Not for any course making purposes, but to let the helmsman sit on the locker that did not contain the fuel for the stove! Apart from this one short tack we were on the same tack for 7 hours. For once we had remembered to close one of the fuel tank taps so the tank which was lower due to our angle of heel did not cross fill from the upper and overflow through the breather tube.

With the stove refuelled it was time to cook a late lunch of beef burgers. Our timing was not the best; we were still heeling so Alison needed to hold the frying pan on the stove, then before they were cooked we came to the end of Eigg and encountered much shorter seas that made balancing a frying pan interesting to say the least! The wind had got up too, and just before the burgers were ready I decided we needed to shorten sail. Alison turned off the stove, and wedged the pan on the floor so it would not spill before heading on deck to take the helm while I dropped the halyards and hauled on the reefing line to put another few turns of sail on the boom. The only yacht that passed us did so at this point, heading straight into the Sound of Sleat.

We talked while we put the reef in, and decided not to try for Canna. The seas were obviously rougher where we were, at the northern end of Eigg, and wind still had too much west in it for a quick passage beating up past Rhum. Our new destination was either Armadale or Isleornsay, which were both inside the shelter of the Sound of Sleat.

With the new destination decided Alison headed back into the cabin, and finished cooking the burgers and fried some onions. There should have been some sliced tomato in the buns too, but it ended up on the floor just after Alison cut it, as a big wave rolled under us. Not a great meal, but wonderful given the conditions it was cooked under!

The seas calmed down soon after that, and we had an easy passage up the sound. Just before Armadale we encountered a trawler on a closing bearing. It was working, so we changed course to clear it, and got a friendly wave as we slowly overtook. The wind increased a little, and when Alison took the helm she got me to lower the stay sail which helped with the weather helm. But an hour later the wind speed had dropped again and backed more westerly. By the time we reached Isleornsay we were on a lovely broad reach.

I wanted to try picking up a mooring under sail, so we sailed into the bay and had a look round. The only visitor's moorings available this year are at Duisdale Hotel. Alison tried calling them up on the VHS, but they did not answer, and none of our mobile phones had any coverage, so we could not phone. Only one of the buoys was in use, so we decided to take one anyway. Alison got the main down and the jib away, and we approached, very slowly, under the stay sail alone. Unfortunately we just failed to make it, so I quickly put the engine on, and five minutes later, at 18:20, we were on the buoy.

We should have gone ashore and patronised the hotel, but after over 10 hours sailing we were both too tired to want to, so I cooked potatoes and heated scotch pies and baked beans and we ate what felt like a feast on board, helped by a small glass of wine each!

The view from the cockpit was gorgeous, but there was hardly any sun, and the wind made it too cold to eat outside. We huddled in the cabin, still wearing all our layers from the day's sailing, bar our jackets. Hopefully we will be warm enough in bed!

Isle Ornsay to Plockton

26/05/2015

The tides through the narrows of Kyle Rhea dictated the best time to leave Isleornsay, so we set the alarm for six, and were off the mooring by half past. The wind was still good for the passage up to Kyle Rhea, so we raised the main, but it was not strong enough to take us up there at a good speed so we motor sailed for a while. The scenery was glorious, but the weather not so good, with only occasional patches of brightness.

We ate some cereal, a real come down from yesterday's porridge, and by the time we were through Kyle Rhea Alison was looking forward to a proper cooked breakfast. We had all the ingredients, so we started talking about where would be the best place to go to eat it. Plockton? Broadford? It would be gone 11 by the time we got to either of them, and there was Kyle of Lochalsh in front of us! The pontoons there are not sheltered from the north west, where the winds were coming from, but we could fill up with diesel and water.

We tied up on an empty pontoon but by the time we finished second breakfast there were two other boats moored with us. We found out that there was water on the pontoon but we would have to carry our cans to the railway pier to get diesel. I spoke to the harbour master there and got some local gossip along with the diesel. The pumps are meant for the fishing fleet and the high pressure nozzles made it hard work for the harbour staff to fill our small cans. We stayed until gone 12, then realised we had to go get a

Gales Every Weekend

move on if we wanted the tide with us under the Skye bridge

We thought about heading to Rona, but the wind was wrong, so we wondered about Loch Torridon. The weather was not encouraging. Cold, damp, and with the wind on the nose! Then the wind shifted for a moment so we could sail, the sky lightened a little, and the afternoon's prospects improved immensely. Alison looked in the Clyde Cruising Club pilot book and found a totally sheltered anchorage in the Crowlins, a trio of islands just off Applecross and we headed there to have a look. It was on the way to Loch Torridon anyway! A small fishing boat waved at us as we got the main down on the approach; it was a friendly wave, but Alison could not tell if he was also telling us to steer clear, or go back!

The Clyde Cruising club said that the anchorage was totally sheltered, but the approach was very narrow, with waves just breaking over submerged rocks at the sides. A couple of seals put their heads out of the water to look at us. A lovely spot, but too narrow for comfort, with hardly any room to swing and it did not feel like a good place to spend the night. We aborted, and decided on an anchorage on the mainland, but as soon as we were out from the shelter of the Crowlins the seas began to roll us around a lot. We got the staysail back up, but it only helped a little, and the heading we needed to reach the other anchorage made the rolling worse. Going back south down the coast, to seek shelter at Plockton, became the best option.

We headed into Loch Carron and found a free visitors mooring at Plockton and were tied up by 1700, and glad to be there. We had the forecast winds of F5-F6 all day, and as soon as we were past the Skye Bridge we got the seas to match. The forecast is pretty much the same, or worse, all week, and then much worse on Sunday through next Tuesday, so we will have to see where we get to!

Sturdy mooring set up

The visitor buoys at Plockton are clearly marked and large, with a good pickup "handbag". These are on thin rope, tied to the loop of long thick rope which is shackled to the buoy; this rope is encased in plastic hose to reduce chafe on the moored boat. The integral loop on the end fitted snugly over *Robinetta's* bits and even though the wind started to howl about 2am we did not worry about staying put.

I was very glad we were in the shelter of Plockton, and when we heard the morning inshore waters forecast from Stornoway Coastguard we decided to stay for a while. We don't mind taking *Robinetta* out in Force 5-7 if we know the seas will be calm, or we know shelter is ahead. We were now in unfamiliar territory and our experience of the Inner Sound yesterday told us that in strong winds the seas here are too rough for comfort in *Robinetta*. The forecast is SW to W, going NW later and staying that way for the next 2 days. Just the wrong directions to get to the Outer Hebrides. There is good phone coverage on the mooring, and I was able to pick up xcweather which gives a longer range information than the Inshore Waters forecast. We might be here for the next six days...

A day in Plockton

27/05/2015

Plockton is a famous yachtman's haunt. It has several highly regarded restaurants and pubs and is well known for Scottish traditional music. Its railway station makes it a popular spot for crew changes. It has a new pontoon but that is really just for the trip boats and landing a dinghy. There is plenty of space to anchor and a large number of well maintained visitors moorings. We spent the day and evening ashore with an excellent pub lunch and a posh dinner followed by a fine music session at the hotel.

Pontoon at Plockton

Rowing back at night the wind was strong. We really only had one chance to grab hold of *Robinetta* as we passed, before getting blown right across Loch Carron. Luckily we made that grab! We had left two of our larger fenders over the side, to stop *Worm* damaging *Robinetta* while we boarded, since they held her far enough away from *Robinetta* to fit our boarding ladder between them. Unfortunately we had not tied one of them on securely enough, and moments after scrambling aboard Alison saw it drifting off into the darkness, an elderly grubby white fender in need of some more air. It would not have been safe in the conditions to chase it in *Worm*, and there were rocks in the direction it headed towards so using *Robinetta* was impossible too.

Up Loch Carron

28/05/2015

Given the forecast we did not have any great expectations of leaving Plockton today, but the bright sun shine gave us hope. When we left the mooring at 10am our plan was to head west, out of Loch Carron, and investigate the sea state. If it was not too bad we would head up to Torridon, but otherwise we would turn straight back, and go for a sail in Loch Carron.

Ten minutes beating out to sea, bashing through short steep waves and watching the white horses get closer made the expected decision simple, we would turn round and go through the Strome narrows and into the shelter of Inner Loch Carron. We tacked rather than gybed *Robinetta* round, then went onto a very broad run back towards Cat Island under the eyes of a seal watch trip boat. Hopefully they got some pictures! The sea state quickly went down, and we had three sails up, so we looked good!

Then we found we didn't really know the way to Inner Loch Carron! Alison found the entrance to the Strome Narrows on the chart and said "follow the trip boat".

We then picked our way through the rocks towards the deep channel to the narrows. I enjoyed this but Alison found it a bit nerve racking. It was all down wind so we needed to gybe several times. We furled away the jib, which meant we only had to worry about the main sail, and got through the "islands" without incident. It was after we entered the main channel, that we relaxed, lost concentration, and had an unplanned gybe, but luckily not an uncontrolled one.

The sea state was slight within the Narrows and we had the tide and wind with us, so made 5½ knots and entered Inner Loch Carron in fine style. Once we were there we got caught by a succession of strong line squalls, some with blindingly heavy rain and some with hail!

There was no fetch so the waves were very slight, but running or broad reaching a gaffer with the wind varying between F2 and F6-7 is 'interesting'. I decided to put an extra reef in the main but by the time we were head to wind I had changed my mind and dropped the main entirely. Then we tried goose winging on staysail and jib but of course the sun came out and the wind died. So up came the main again, with the extra reef. It was so nice Alison went below to put the kettle on.

Upper Loch Carron, looking back at the narrow entrance

Then the next squall hit. "Can you come up and furl the jib?" I called down. Alison secured the kettle and leap up but the wind was so strong the jib used up all the furling line and was only half away. I put the helm over to let the mainsail shield the jib from the wind and Alison let it out and put it away again, successfully, this time. To kill the power I dropped the peak and we sailed on with staysail and saggy peak until the squall was over. Then the sun came out again and we had our cup of tea. They do some powerful squalls in Loch Carron.

Somewhere along the way we did another good gybe and then I lost concentration and the boom went back over again. The back-stays are wire rope down to a wooden block, then a rope through the block is used to tension the leeward back-stay. The blocks are at just the right height for the boom to hit them on a gybe. The roller reefing means that with a reef in the sail gets crushed between the boom and the block. Another hole that will need mending this winter.

Gales Every Weekend

Sgeir Fhada, with Slumbay Harbour behind, Upper Loch Carron

After that things calmed down for a bit. I looked on my tablet and found that there is an Antares chart for the rocks at the top of the loch and Slumbay Harbour. These large scale charts give a lot of detail, which made it safe to take *Robinetta* right up to the top and round Sgeir Fhada (the well named 'long rock' – it looks like a shingle bank). Of course we had to put the engine on at the end of the loch as the return trip was head to wind all the way.

The wind was really strong as we stowed the main and motored to the harbour. There were a few good empty moorings – ideal for a lunch stop and to wait for the tide to turn in the Narrows. Picking one up was another matter – the wind kept pushing us away. Alison managed to get the boat hook onto one buoy but could not haul it close enough to get a line on. Then the boat hook would not come free and got snatched out of her hand, only to free itself from the buoy and sink straight to the bottom.

Time to try an alternative method. We motored past a buoy and I got a rope around it from the cockpit and then Alison walked the rope to the bow and tied a bowline bridle round the samson posts. We went below for a light lunch and were cosy inside when the biggest squall hit with heavy rain that turned into hail.

The return trip was uneventful but as we got out of the Narrows the wind in the outer loch had freshened quite a bit. There were white horses and the spray was getting blown off the tops, even though the waves, luckily, were still low and far enough apart that we could keep above 2 knots under engine. It was windy enough even at Plockton that it took two goes to pick up a mooring, this time using the short boat hook which is all we have left until we can get to a chandlers. As we got the jib down and the sail covers on I spotted a broad rainbow over the Strome narrows. A pretty end to an interesting sail, but it was time to put our feet up!

Weather Window, Plockton to Loch Hourn

29/05/2015

The next two days promise a lull before a gale on Sunday. We looked for the best place to sit out the bad weather, and decided on Mallaig as having the best shelter for the expected wind direction. We dropped the mooring buoy in bright sunshine and headed over to the pontoon in *Robinetta*. We needed to put a cheque in the honesty box to pay for the mooring, and Alison did not fancy another row over in *Worm*. We had the lines and fenders all set, but as we approached we were warned off the only empty spot as the trip boat was going to come alongside. It was not a problem, as the people keeping the pontoon clear were happy to take the envelope so Alison reached out and handed it over from the cockpit as we passed.

Alison took the helm and I raised the main while still in the shelter of the bay as I had yesterday, but today there was no turning back; the sea was slight, and we sailed west on a fine reach, heading for Kyle of Lochalsh. The wind was light, then went lighter. We took the reef out for the first time this trip, and I decided to change up from the No 2 jib.

The Skye Bridge from the north

There were black clouds and heavy rain over Skye, and by the time the number 1 jib was ready to use the clouds were nearly on top of us. Alison didn't want to unfurl the jib until the next tack, and we were glad of that when the squall hit. We went from 1 knot to 5 in 30 seconds, heeling well over until Alison came off the wind and let out the main. I quickly put the reef back in!

The squall passed as quickly as it had arrived, and the wind died away as we went under the Skye Bridge. A fishing boat coming up behind us was very understanding as we lost steerage way and drifted across his path before Alison could get the engine on! We got the main down and motored to the Kyle of Lochalsh pontoon for a late lunch stop.

Once tied up we went of in search of lunch. Hector's Bothy did a good fish and chips. Then we headed for the local hardware store; it used to be called Marine Stores, but had recently changed its name. We did not hope for much, as it contained standard home decorating/maintenance stuff, but we asked if they happened to have a boat hook anyway. Sorry, no boat hooks, but they did have a galvanised iron boat hook head, and broom handles. We could managed with that. We had a long chat with the ex-fisherman who served us, then headed back to *Robinetta*.

entrance to Loch Hourn

I spent the rest of the afternoon putting the new boat hook together while Alison did various boat chores, then we cast off at 16:30, heading for Kyle Rhea on stay sail and jib. We were only making 2-3 knots but were not in a hurry as the tide would not turn in our favour until 17:30. Once at the entrance to the narrows we furled the jib and went through on engine. We got a good boost through, making 5-7 knots. There were some swirly bits on the south end, but no overfalls or rips. In fact there was very little wind in the Sound of Sleet. We kept the stay sail up, but did not bother raising any other sails.

We could have gone all the way to Mallaig, but decided to have a look inside Loch Hourn. An excellent decision! We followed the Clyde Cruising Club directions to a sheltered anchorage behind Eilean Rarsaidh, and spent a peaceful night in beautiful surroundings.

Better weather, Loch Hourn to Mallaig

30/05/2015

We had a lovely quiet night in the anchorage and woke to spectacular views. After a light breakfast I took *Worm* out to take some pictures.

Landing on the island was difficult because of the bladderwrack, but I did get a better shot of the bluebell wood from Worm.

Eilean Rarsaidh, Loch Hourn

On the mainland shore the rocky outcrop had one good landing spot and from the top I could get decent zoom shots of *Robinetta* although the light wasn't really right.

Back aboard it was time to haul up the anchor. We had a lot of chain out but with no wind or tide to pull us backwards the hauling was easy; the anchor came up really clean too! Exploring the upper loch would have been nice, but we could not get the latest weather forecast at the anchorage, and the expected strong winds might arrive earlier than we knew, so heading straight for Mallaig was the sensible option. Once we were clear of the shelter what wind there was was not favourable so we motored out of Loch Hourn and then motor sailed to Mallaig.

We got there around 2 pm and suddenly it was hot and sunny. We picked a pontoon berth where we thought we would not get blown on when the gale came, and tied up, then lifted *Worm* out of the water and onto the end of the pontoon before going for lunch.

Later, I finally got to refit the missing quarter knee to *Worm* and reattach the loose thwart, while Alison put a coat of varnish on the new boat hook to stop it getting mouldy in the damp locker.

Storm Bound in Mallaig

01/06/2015

Mallaig Marina is not really finished yet, even though the pontoons have been available since 2013. The shower/toilet block is still being built, so not "available 2015" as advertised, but there are showers in the old seaman's mission, and decent public toilets no further from the pontoons than in a large marina. The shelter is also much better than we feared, and we have been comfortable here so far. When we arrived on Saturday lunchtime there was plenty of space, but it has been slowly filling. There are now 3 boats chartered from Armadale sitting out the gales here, and when *Eda Fransen* arrived yesterday, she reported a 52 knot gust out in the bay...

We had lost a fender at the end of last year, then another one at Plockton, which left us only three decent size ones, so we were short of fenders to put between *Robinetta* and the pontoon if the wind started blowing her on. We decided we should buy a couple.

The chandler/hardware store at Kyle of Lochalsh had not have any fenders obviously for sale and we forgot to ask, so we went to the chandlers in Mallaig. They had none on display either, but they were much more obviously a chandlers, set up for big fishing boat supplies with a good supply of shackles and the first galvanised blocks I've seen on sale. We asked, and they did carry fenders, so one of the men behind the counter walked us to their storage shed and asked what size we wanted then inflated two for us. We fitted them to *Robinetta* immediately, against the changeable winds expected in the evening. She had been blown off the pontoon by the winds so far, but the winds were forecast to swing all over the place later, so the extra fenders were necessary.

We also bought some more shock cord to make dampers for *Robinetta*'s shore lines. Hopefully they will make for a quieter night tonight than yesterday.

Mallaig to Inverie, Knoydart

02/06/2015

After the gale we have a weather window between now (Tuesday) and next Saturday, when the winds will "only" be F4-6. It will take time for the sea state to go down, so today we decided not to try to get to Canna, but to have a short sail into Loch Nevis and pick up a mooring at the Old Forge Inn at Inverie. It took time to prepare for sea after being battened down against the gales in harbour, but we *thought* we were ready (full water tanks, full diesel, anchor lashed to the bulwarks, bowsprit out with no 2 jib), so set off out of the harbour at 11:40.

We were clear of the harbour, in a fair amount of swell, when Alison realised that the boom was still in its crutches. In still water this would not be a problem, but untying the crutches, then pulling up the topping lifts while *Robinetta* is being flung abruptly up and down is far from simple, and I could not keep my footing as I tried to raise the boom. We headed back into the shelter of the harbour, with Alison holding the boom off with one hand while helming through the swell with the other. I had taken the forward sail tie off too, so with the topping lifts/ lazy jacks loose there was a bag of main sail free to catch the wind, We sailed on that, and the already raised stay sail, and made good time back into harbour!

I got the main lifted up out of the way, and spotted our second mistake. Alison had shackled the jib the wrong way round on the Wykeham-Martin gear so it could not unfurl. I went forward and fixed it. Once that was sorted I raised the main sail and we sailed back out towards Loch Nevis.

After the drama at the beginning of the sail we had a lovely very broad reach into Loch Nevis, almost surfing down the waves. We got half a mile from the moorings, and decided that we had not really sailed enough, so we headed further up the Loch towards the narrows. This meant coming much closer to the wind. It felt colder immediately, and after about ten minutes we decided to head back to the moorings, pick one up, and go for a walk.

The Old Forge Inn at Inverie is in the Guinness Book Of World Records as the most remote pub in mainland Britain. There is an old road to Kinlochhourn but it was never adapted for motor traffic and is now designated a 'rural path'. On the other hand it has a frequent ferry service from Mallaig so it is easier to get to by public transport than many other places.We first went there many years ago in *Ariel of Hamble* and it is a famous sailor's haunt. There are supposed to be 11 visitor moorings but the marina master at Mallaig had warned us that they had not been checked since the new owner took over. Alison could only count six of the uniform type we expect of visitor moorings, but we were the only yacht any where near and there was plenty of space.

We furled the jib away and lowered the main, then sailed onto the mooring on stay sail. I managed a perfect approach and Alison had no problems using our new boat hook to pick up the mooring line, even though it had no pick up buoy on it.

Alison rowed us shore, and we went to the inn to book our dinner (and tell them we were on their mooring) then went for a lovely walk.

We ate dinner looking out at the moorings, and noticed a buoy that seemed different from the others, just inshore of the one that *Robinetta* was on. We were pretty sure it had not been there when we arrived! When it disappeared we assumed it had been a seal. Once we were back on board *Robinetta* Alison noticed something in the same spot again. We were much closer this time and could see it properly. An otter! The first we've seen. Gavin Maxwell lived with Mijbil the otter at the entrance to Loch Hourn, 9 miles north, and wrote of his experiences in the book Ring of Bright Water; seeing an otter here felt special.

Inverie

The mooring is not especially sheltered and we are rolling a bit, but it is not too bad and we will be able to stay here over night comfortably enough. The views from the cockpit are certainly worth a bit of rolling!

Inverie to Canna

03/06/2015

We had a disturbed night, with squalls that set *Worm* jumping up and down. We had tied her up alongside, something we often do it the wind and tide are not in agreement, but Alison got up in the night to free her off and then was up again half an hour later to bring her back alongside. Not a good night! We prepared to go early, then stopped to make and eat porridge, and left the mooring at 08:30.

We had a slow beat out of Loch Nevis even though we shook out the reef, then a slow beat across the Sound of Sleat, then a slow beat up the South end of Skye. As we cleared Skye the seas got up a bit, but we were half way along the coast of Rhum before we gave in and put on the engine. There was enough wind to sail (we even put the reef back in) but the sea state was such that *Robinetta* kept being stopped by the waves, and the engine helped her power through them. The whole trip got less frustrating at that point and we kept the engine on most of the rest of the way.

Head winds all day, and an ETA at Canna that went from 18:08 to 19:58 could have made for a depressing sail, but the weather was fine, with plenty of blue sky and sun. The waves were occasionally unpleasant, but never dangerous, and so long as we were in the shelter of Rhum it was really rather nice!

Leaving Loch Nevis

The last five miles from Rhum to Canna were the most exposed of the trip, and beating against the headwind meant we sailed at least 7 miles, and probably 8, but we did not mind because half way across we were surrounded by a pod of dolphins. They rode our bow wave, powered along side, jumped out of the water... Whenever we tacked they lost us for a couple of minutes, then powered back to catch up again. It was a lovely sight!

We lowered the sails before entering Canna harbour and picked up a mooring. There are ten visitor moorings here, and there were already 7 yachts. Not bad for a midweek in June! It feels much more sheltered than Inverie though, and Alison expects to sleep like a log.

Canna to Eriskay

04/06/2015

Ferry quay at Canna

This time we had a beautifully peaceful night, with *Worm* hanging off the back as though she would never dream of knocking on the transom! A slight swell began just after we got up, encouraging us to leave. Last night's forecast had been "variable". After a day of head winds I said "Any where from south west to north west will get us to the Outer Hebrides so let's go on whatever heading is good for sailing".

We raised sail in the bay and tried to sail out, but were headed, so put the engine on again. Things felt better when we were out past the rocks and we were able to turn onto a broad reach. We headed up along the north coast of Canna and with the wind in the south-east we could lay a course to almost any point in the Outer Hebrides! We decided to head for Castlebay on Barra. From there we could head north towards the new marina at Lochboisdale to sit out the bad weather that was due on Saturday.

We had a lovely broad reach for the first couple of hours, but then had to pull the jib in a bit as the wind went round. Not a problem! Some days are perfect for sailing, and this was one of them. All the frustration of beating against head winds yesterday disappeared as *Robinetta* ate up the miles on one long reach. Every now and then a roller would push us off course, and we had to watch the steering, especially for the first five miles when we could not see anything ahead, but as soon as we had something to point at helming got simpler.

Then we picked up the new forecast, and had to change our minds about where we should go. Castlebay is exposed to the South west, and the new forecast had South force 6 later, which meant we could expect a bumpy night. We started to head towards Lochboisdale, but then I spotted that the harbour on Eriskay, which has two visitor moorings, was totally protected. This only needed a small course change, and was no further than Barra or Lochboisdale, so off we went.

The weather was cold, and we only saw scraps of blue sky but it was a bright dry day. And great sailing. We sailed right into Arcaseid Mor, gaelic for "big harbour", through its twisty entrance, and picked up a buoy under sail. It was not our most elegant try at this (two passes, and we ended up picking up a different buoy to the one we first chose) but we were tied up by 16 20. We have reached the Outer Hebrides!

Arcaseid Mor, Eriskay

We were planning to head straight to Lochboisdale tomorrow, so decided we had to land on Eriskay this evening despite the clouds dropping lower, threatening rain. After rowing to the fishing boat pontoon we walked up the hill, aiming for the A M Politician, the local pub named after the boat that sank off Eriskay and inspired the book and film "Whisky Galore".

We managed to get to the Co-op before it closed and stocked up on bread, milk, and veg, then on to the pub for dinner.

Eriskay to Lochboisdale

05/06/2015

We accidentally slept through the 07:10 forecast, and the steady rain on the cabin roof did not encourage us to move, so we had a slow start to the day. We only wanted to to go the few miles to Lochboisdale to sit out Saturday/Sunday's gale, so there seemed no particular rush. We did make sure we listened to the 10:10 repeat of the forecast, and suddenly we were in a hurry. The gale would be arriving earlier than expected, with winds reaching force 7 by lunchtime. Eriskay harbour might be beautifully protected, but again, neither of us wanted to be on a mooring, possibly stranded there by too much wind to row ashore, for three nights!

We prepared to go in the rain, raising the mainsail and reefing it right down by untying the first hoop, and pulling in every inch of reef we could. We also raised the staysail before casting off from the buoy. We did not try to sail out though as the entrance channel is quite twisty, (one reason for the excellent shelter).

The seas outside felt high as we cleared the entrance and we began to roll. There was a snapping sound, and Alison glanced up to the gaff and saw that the out-haul - the line that pulls the sail back along the spar and keeps it tight - had broken, leaving the sail sliding forward along the gaff.

We then had a rather uncomfortable ten minutes getting the main down as *Robinetta* rolled violently. Alison helmed while I wrestled with the sail. We had to turn head to wind to get the sail down, but we were still too close to the rocky entrance for comfort, so Alison could not motor forward fast enough to keep her head to wind constantly as the swell pushed us from side to side.

After we got the mainsail down we decided to motor to Lochboisedale rather than try to fix the out-haul, since it was not far away. As we got further out to sea the waves became more comfortable and Alison could turn onto our best course clear of Eriskay, with the waves coming from astern. *Robinetta* was much more comfortable on that heading, although she still needed careful helming when occasional waves came at her sideways. The wind was not too strong, and the staysail flopped from side to side as *Robinetta* descended into the troughs of the waves, but Alison soon got the hang of the wave patterns and the rolling became less, and the staysail kept her steadier.

The rain stopped. Blue sky appeared and *Worm* followed along behind on a long line without problems. The swell got worse as we approached Rubha na h'Ordaig, the headland just south of Lochboisdale, and I checked the

Gales Every Weekend

Clyde Cruising Club Pilot. It suggested we leave it a mile to port! Luckily we did not need to go that far out for the waves to decrease, but it was a reminder that we should not get complacent. The wind began to pick up, and we were glad of the shelter of Rubha na h'Ordaig after we rounded it and headed into Lochboisdale.

The marina has just been opened, and has space for 52 boats, but there are few resident vessels so it was mostly empty as we came in just after 13 00, and we had our pick of berths. The wind was definitely on the rise, and we got *Robinetta* and *Worm* ready for the gale, then went for a shower. The first in six days. Heaven!

Later, I checked the gaff out-haul. The line had chafed through and just tying it back would give us the same problem again later. Also the solid plug of wood in the end of the hollow gaff was loose, so some thinking was required. We went ashore, looking for some Wi-Fi, and found it at a lovely coffee shop cum Post- Office.

Lochboisdale Marina

Sitting out the gale in Lochboisedale Harbour

05/06/2015

Robinetta is creaking against her lines, but the shock cord loops are doing a great job of damping the motion. We started with shock cord on the fore and aft main mooring lines, but the stern was taking very little strain compared to the bow, so I moved the shock cord to the second bow line instead, the one holding the bow away from the finger berth. This is not a line we usually deploy, (we did not use one in Mallaig) but the shelter from the marina walls decreased noticeably as the tide came in during the evening, and *Robinetta* moved more.

Worm is on the pontoon, upside-down. There are no boats moored past us on this arm of the marina, so she is not in anyone's way and it is much better for her than being in the water, Gusts run across the water raising angry ripples and mini waves, while beyond the sheltering arms of the entrance there are white horses despite the short fetch in the Loch.

Walking along the pontoon towards the shower block requires care; the brand new pontoons are wide, with good traction, but the wind is so strong that leaning into it becomes automatic, and it could blow a child over and off into the water in an instant. There are no children here though. The seven other sailing yachts and one motor yacht are all crewed by adults. *Robinetta* is the smallest, but probably the one riding out the gale with the least fuss. Her mast is shorter, so gets caught less by the wind, and she sits lower in the water than the other yachts, despite her high cabin sides, so dances less in the gusts. At 22:20, as Alison was writing up the log, I found weather stations on the web saying the wind speed in the last ten minutes has been 23 mph gusting 41. Alison says she's glad to be in harbour, and on a pontoon with no worries about rowing ashore! I think so too.

Tomorrow we will catch a bus, and explore on land!

North Uist, by Bus

06/06/2015

We bought a book of walks in the Outer Hebrides in the Co-op at Eriskay, and the one that really caught my eye was on North Uist. A check of the bus timetable revealed that we could catch a bus to the start point, and have two hours to do the walk (timetabled at 1 hour) We are not slow walkers, but we do like to take our time at the places on the way, so this seemed to be excellent timing.

Gales Every Weekend

The bus started from Lochboisdale so we had no problems catching it. It was quite a long trip from the South end of South Uist, then across Benbecula and half way up North Uist, but it meant we saw bits of the archipelago that we would otherwise miss. There were several people aboard the bus when we left Lochboisdale, but by the time we reached North Uist we had it to ourselves.

The bus dropped us at the entrance to the Barpa Langass chambered cairn. Unfortunately the chamber has been closed off after a rock fall, but we took a good took at it from the outside, then headed for the nearest trig point. The view was spectacular!

the head of Loch Langais from above Pobull Fhinn

We then went down hill to the Pobull Fhinn, the only stone circle on North Uist. It was rather wet underfoot, and we were glad of our boots, but the way was well marked, and we had no problems following it with the help of our guide book.

Then it was back to the road in good time to catch the bus.

On the way back we stopped off at the South Uist museum and craft centre for a bite to eat. We had seen a boat sitting outside it as we passed it heading north, and Alison thought it it looked familiar.

Back in the 1990s Alison took me to the London Boat Show at Earl's Court, to see the Lord of the Isles Galley, *Aileach*. That visit was the start of the family interest in sailing, and here lay *Aileach* again. One of her planks is cracked, and she is on display while the trust that owns her raises money for repairs.

Our third bus of the day returned us to Lochboisdale. It was early enough that the village hardware store was still open. I bought some PVA glue and stuck the plug back in the end of the gaff, before we headed to the very old fashioned Lochboisdale Hotel for dinner. This caters mainly to the fishermen who come to South Uist for fly fishing, and the food was not to my taste.

Aileach ashore

Lochboisedale to Lochmaddy

07/06/2015

The wind was still blowing hard when we woke in the morning. The 07:10 forecast sounded hopeful but we had a lie in and then pottered about waiting for the wind to drop. There was one essential job to do before we could leave. The glue seems to have worked a treat on the gaff end-plug. I untied the broken out-haul line and brought it below. We had only lost about 18" so I cut, heat sealed, and served the broken end.

I didn't want to just tie the sail back on, since if the line chafed once it would do it again. I found a piece of threaded rod - the same type we use to bolt the spar-end to the gaff. It fitted the hole in the gaff perfectly, tapping itself in. I cut it to length and screwed it in, using mole grips to twist it until about

3/4" poked out each side, then wormed the thread on the ends with serving twine before parcelling them with gaffer tape and serving them with tarred marlin. That made a nice smooth cleat that will not slide or put load on the inside of the hole.

The wind was still blowing but I took off the sail cover and ties then raised the gaff a few inches to tie the out-haul round the new cleat. We were a sailing boat again! We got the No. 2 jib on and untied the two extra shore lines so we just had bow, stern and springs. We were being blown strongly onto the pontoon.

There is a weather station quite near that publishes to the internet. It was reading 12 mph gusting 18, much gentler than it felt in harbour, so it we seemed to be in a blowy part of the island. We debated with the boat next to us - they were off to Barra via Eriskay. About 12:30 we decided to poke our nose out. Our berth companion did a sterling job of pushing *Robinetta* away from the pontoon as we motored out. In the outer loch we turned towards the wind to raise sail but had to wait a moment to let a fishing boat past before raising the deeply reefed main.

Ushenish Lighthouse

The wind blew mostly west giving us a nice close reach along the coast and the seas were really slight. Throughout the day we had periods when fronts went overhead and the wind got flaky but mostly we sailed steadily at 4 1/2 to 5 knots. It went light enough that we shook out some reef and tied the bottom hoop back on and fitted the No. 1 jib but the gusts were strong enough were were both happier leaving some reef in.

Ushenish Lighthouse plagued us for what seemed like hours. It felt like we couldn't get past it. We dropped below 2 knots and then got back up to 4 but we still seemed stuck. It just took patience though and once past we picked up speed again and had a fantastic sail with plenty of blue sky between the cloud fronts. The coastline is quite fine along both Uists but very flat past Benbecula.

As we neared Madagh Mhor I looked to find the entrance to Loch Eport - the stone circle we walked to is at the head of the loch. The entrance is invisible until it is abeam and then it stands out clearly as a complete hole in the coastline! Madagh Mhor itself is an impressive site. Almost vertically sided on the west and sloping on the east.

We lost the wind as we neared it and went between it and the mainland under motor. Once through and round the headland we were perfectly head to wind and had just the right amount of time before reaching Loch Maddy harbour to drop the main, shake all the reef out and flake it nicely on the boom.

Madagh Mhor at the entrance to Loch Maddy

The ferry startled us a bit, deciding to leave just as we approached the harbour, but it took the other channel out. Both visitors moorings were taken but there was plenty of space on the brand new pontoons. A lady from another yacht took our line as we moored - they had seen us in Canna but came straight to Lochmaddy and have been here ever since. One of the great things about a distinctive boat is being remembered by people you meet elsewhere.

It was about 20:30. We were both too tired to want to explore so Alison stayed outside to put covers on while I cooked. The cupboard was a bit bare but I found garlic, onions, tomatoes and sweet peppers and I suddenly discovered I was making piperade. We eat that with tuna at home so I went looking for some fish. Alison remembered buying a tin of eel in some kind of sauce and we found it. It turned the piperade into a delicious slightly Chinese tasting antipasto which we followed with penne pasta in a tomato and wild mushroom sauce (courtesy of Mr Grossman). I had a bottle of Skye Red ale and Alison had red wine. I think we set a better table than some establishments, even when the larder is bare!

Lochmaddy to Plocrapool

08/06/2015

After a morning of shopping, museum visiting and blogging we left Lochmaddy at 13:00. It was another cold and damp day, but with a good sailing wind and calm seas. Once again, after the sails were up, we did not need to tack, but stayed on port tack, with various sail sets all the way up the coast. We kept quite close in until we got to the end of North Uist so had good views of the coast. Once passing the Sound of Harris we headed directly for East Loch Tarbert. Visibility decreased as we got further off shore, and thick cloud often hid South Harris, meaning we needed a compass course rather than aiming for a headland.

Our speed was generally good, with 5 knots in the gusts, and never dropping below 3½ knots, so it was a good sailing day but the weather was pretty dreary. We had a lovely five minutes when we were in a patch of sun shine, but that was all.

We had been thinking of anchoring at Scoravik on the east side of Scalpay (a large island in the entrance to East Loch Tarbert), but the wind backed a little, and threatened to go round further which would have put us on a run, which is not a relaxing point of sail. In order to make sure the wind stayed on the beam we shifted our destination to Plocrapool inside East Loch Tarbert. It looks scary on our GPS charts, but the Antares Charts surveyed it last summer, and using them took the worry out of the "uncharted rocks" danger area of our other charts!

We dropped the anchor exactly as recommended by Antares, which does feel close to the rocks, but the anchor is holding well, and it is very sheltered. Anchoring always feels like an adventure, but the Clyde Cruising Club pilots, and the Antares charts take the worry out of it.

East Loch Tarbert, Harris, and the Shaints

09/06/2015

After a lovely peaceful night in Plocrapool it was time to up the anchor and head further up the Loch for provisions. It was only about 3 miles to East Loch Tarbert, so we could have just motored, but with a lovely wind just outside the shelter of the anchorage I wanted to sail. After hauling up the anchor and stowing it we turned back to get the main up inside the anchorage. A surprised seal fell off the tiny pinnacle of rock it had been hauled out on as we changed course in front of it. Until Alison heard the splash she had thought it was a rock itself!

Once clear of the rocks the engine went off, and we had a lovely sail up to East Loch Tarbert. There used to be visitor's moorings there, but they have gone, and now everyone needs to anchor. Alison laid out fifteen meters of chain on the deck and dropped anchor quite close inshore to be out of the ferry's turning circle.

Anchored at East Loch Tarbert

We rowed ashore in Worm to check out Tarbert. It has a few good shops, the biggest being the Harris Tweed shop. A distillery is being built next to the Tweed shop. We walked half mile across the isthmus to West Loch Tarbert. There are some nice hotels along the way.

Then it was back to East Loch Tarbert for shopping, and brunch at a lovely coffee shop, before rowing back to *Robinetta* to up anchor again. The ferry was in, but seemed to be having problems, so although it was fully loaded even before we got back on board *Robinetta* it stayed put. The bow doors were open, but it was using its bow thrusters, the back wash from which sent *Robinetta* dancing round her anchor in an interesting way! We were glad to get clear.

We got the main and staysail up, but left the jib (no1) furled as we were sailing on a virtually dead run. A gust came, and *Robinetta* set off like a scalded cat. Alison found her difficult to hold, so we went head to wind and reefed away a couple of rolls of sail round the boom. There were no problems after that as we sailed under Scalpay bridge and set course for the Shiants.

Sailing beneath the Scalpay Bridge

Alison was expecting to need to reef more when clear of Scalpay but the wind was steady and the waves just gave a nice gentle roll from the stern quarter. We had a glorious very broad reach all the way across the Little Minch, making 5½ knots on reefed main. We both wanted to see the Shiants. They have been on our radar since we read Adam Nicolson's book 'Sea Room'.

Initially I set a course for the recommended entry from the south; there are overfalls marked but they are a good way south of the islands. Then the wind backed and it looked easier to make for the north end. The tide runs up to 3 knots through the narrows but it is the standard way in from Stornoway. Then the wind veered again and we ended up at the south end after all.

There are three main islands in the Shiants, Eilean an Tighe (house island), Eilean Garbh (rough island) and Eilean Mhuire (Mary's island). The first two are actually joined together. A stack heads out west from Eilean Garbh. It was stunning with terns, cormorants, fulmars, guillemots and puffins out in force. Both sky and sea were thick with birds.

As we rounded Eilean an Tighe the sea got up as we entered an area with overfalls, which were closer in than marked on the chart. The wind was stronger than we had hoped too. The cliff is an incredible display of columnar basalt, painted with lichen, and decorated with nesting birds.

I was afraid the wind would blow straight across the isthmus where the normal anchorage is and I was proven right. I had hoped the alternative northern anchorage would be calmer but there was swell in the whole bay and the wind seemed to be blowing down the steep slope of Eilean Garbh. We knew it did in strong winds but had hoped for calm weather.

With strong but slightly flaky winds coming off the cliffs and across the isthmus it was difficult to look round, so Alison turned *Robinetta* head to wind and put the engine on while I got the main sail down.

Once *Robinetta* was under easy control we explored the bay between Eilean an Tighe, and Garbh Eilean. Staying overnight had always been dependant on how the anchorage felt, and we both decided that we would rather not risk it. It felt a shame to leave the birds, but we got the main back up and set off towards the mainland through the north entrance. Alison was tired - she had helmed all the way from Tarbert and didn't want to stop, but it was time so she handed the helm over.

Gales Every Weekend

North East corner of Garbh Eilean, Shiants

Leaving the Shiants was disappointing but the right decision. I had made sure there was a plan B and Loch Shell was less than two hours away. Outside the narrows we really got into overfalls and the wind was nasty too, and we had an uncomfortable ten minutes before things settled down.

After a while Alison noticed the sails were set very badly. I told her I was tired too and had de-powered the rig for a rest. That wasn't getting us where we needed to go. We unfurled the jib, trimmed the sails, and picked back up to 4-5 knots heading towards Loch Shell. The sun shone on Lewis, and then on us, so we had a lovely sail back across the Little Minch. Once in the shelter of Loch Shell we were soon getting the sails down to pick a careful path through rocks to an anchorage tucked in behind Eilean Luphard, north west of Sgier Ghlas.

Anchoring two nights in a row, with a brunch anchorage thrown in, has certainly given us both practice. So far the fisherman's anchor has worked well for us. We put out 3-4 times the scope of chain (sometimes 5 if we are feeling anxious), and have not dragged once.

Loch Shell to Stornoway

10/06/2015

Last night's anchorage was not as flat calm as Plocrapool, but we only rolled a little bit in the gusts, and *Worm* stayed solidly out of the way on her rope off *Robinetta's* stern. A bit of kelp came up on the anchor chain, and Alison needed a little engine assist to help break out the anchor, but nothing major.

Still up at the bow Alison noticed the Wykeham-Martin gear had no spare turns on it, so she put some on by hand before raising the no 1 jib. This turned out to be a bad idea as she wound them on the "wrong" way so the job unfurled itself as she hoisted it. It had to come down again, the Wykeham-Martin drum reloaded, then the jib hoisted. By the time Alison had done all this we were at the entrance to Loch Shell and beginning to roll in the sea swell. She had been planning to raise the main as well (I've done it every time this trip) but she was struggling and I took pity on her, and handed over the tiller. Alison turned back into the loch to go head to wind for me to haul the main up. Then we headed out towards the sea.

The course towards Stornoway was a dead run, and there was a lot of swell to make the boom rise, but once we rigged a preventer all the fears of an accidental gybe disappeared and we had a lovely sail up the coast.

Back in Mallaig Alison had bought a snap shackle, and I spliced a rope round it with a thimble. The idea was to use this as a mooring line, but the snap shackle turned out to be too small to fit on to the massive rings on the local mooring buoys. However the rope and shackle turned out to be a good piece of kit to use as a preventer, with the rope tied round the boom and the shackle clipped onto the shrouds. This was much easier to disengage than a rope tied both ends.

Once round Kebock Head we were able to gybe *Robinetta* onto the port tack and by the time we passed the entrance to Loch Erisort the wind had come round enough for us to be on a broad reach rather than a run. Approaching Stornoway the wind strengthened, and we thought about reefing, but we did not have far to go and I was enjoying holding the helm against the wind. We did furl the jib away though, and were still doing 5 knots.

We lowered the main just opposite the ferry dock, as that stretch of water was head to wind, then motored towards the marina. Alison called the harbour on the VHF, and for this first time this cruise there was someone there to answer! We were directed to a berth, and helped into it by the crew of the *Norman James*. We had seen them in Canna and Lochboisdale, and talked to them in Lochmaddy. Now we met them again for the last time as they head towards Orkney tomorrow.

Stornoway marina seems like a good place. There are well places cleats on the pontoons, good showers, and plenty of local amenities. Tomorrow is a shore exploration day!

Days in Stornoway

12/06/2015

Stornoway is a great place from which to explore Harris and Lewis, so we hired a car while *Robinetta* sat in the marina, sporting a few new patches of grey metallic primer. She is looking much shabbier this year than last, mostly because we did not have enough time to get her ready. Hopefully the grey metallic will stop water getting under more of the paintwork and increasing next winter's work!

Meanwhile I drove us to all places we would have loved to have sailed to if the weather had been co-operative for more of the time. We headed north first, making for the northern tip of Lewis.

Our first stop was the Butt of Lewis, which is officially the windiest place in the UK. The light house has been converted, so it is automated and no longer has a traditional Fresnel lens.

The cliffs are spectacular. From some aspects there is a weird optical

Looking north from the Butt of Lewis

illusion where the left hand bay looks about 300 feet below the level of the water to the right of it and the far right ocean looks even higher. It doesn't show in the pictures.

Even on the calm day we had, the surf is impressive.

I took lots of pictures of the wildlife with my new camera. The 30x zoom enables some great shots and the distortion doesn't seem bad at all. Then we got back into the car and headed south to Dun Carloway Broch.

It was interesting to compare this with the ones on Orkney. The basic idea is very similar, but different sites bring different issues, and there were no obvious buildings outside Dun Carloway, unlike the Broch of Gurness. The inside was larger, and the presence of openings from the intrawall stairs into the main area made it obvious that people did move around inside the walls.

The best known tourist destination on Lewis are the stone circles at Callanish. There are three circles although most people only visit Callanish I, the largest, where the interpretation centre is located.

Callanish I

We had our lunch there, but did not bother to go into the display area. Callanish I is as impressive as Alison had hoped, and while it is possible to walk from there to the other two circles we decided to drive to save time.

Callanish II is much smaller than the main circle, but with equally impressive views and beautiful stones. We had the place to ourselves, unlike at the main circle. I went back to the car as my boots were rubbing and Alison walked on to the third circle. This was smaller again, but very atmospheric.

Then it was back to the car to head south again, to visit Great Bernera. This is the main island in the beautiful Loch Rog. The Iron Age house reconstruction at Bosta has a thatched roof in most photos online but they have now replaced it with turf as the thatch was only lasting a couple of years. There was a guide inside to talk about the reconstruction and the site, and she also had lamps and a peat fire burning to give an idea of what it would have been like to live there.

Gales Every Weekend

Iron Age house at Bosta, Great Bernera

Our last stop was at Skebadale Bay, which is gorgeous, and very close to where the Lewis Chessmen were found. We saw a huge bird overhead here, and are pretty certain it was a golden eagle, but unfortunately got no pictures.

I totalled up our three week trip. *Robinetta* (and *Worm*) have travelled 282 nm in 91 hours under way, 32 of those with the engine on. We only made one passage on engine alone - the short hop from Kyle Rhea to Loch Hourn. We did motor sail now and again but unlike last year, most passages were sailed. We spent 8 days ashore either stormbound or sightseeing. Despite the weather we made full use of our time and achieved all our main objectives.

We had been planning to leave *Robinetta* in Stornoway Marina. Alison had phoned back in May to check that there were no rules on how long visitors could stay. They had been fine with it, but now we were there the marina attendants wanted to know who would be keeping an eye on the boat, as it was not their job. This seemed odd, boats are left unattended in marinas all the time! We had made a few friends on the pontoon. *Worm* caught some eyes and I helped out with internet access for an old laptop. We asked if anyone knew someone who could keep an eye on *Robinetta* to keep the marina happy.

We were introduced to Ken Linklater who runs the local moorings society, and he suggested that we might be better on a mooring belonging to a friend of his. The boat that normally used that mooring would be elsewhere for the month that we needed it, and it was in a well sheltered part of the harbour. The owner had dived on it to check it in the spring, and Ken gave us very detailed advice on how to approach it and which bit of the bay to stay clear of. Perfect! A wooden boat is always better on a swinging mooring than on a pontoon, as the drying effect of the sun is spread more evenly.

Ken also invited us to a ceilidh which was held on a visiting French boat. We had a great time, with music and chat!

Early next morning we motored *Robinetta* round to the bay on the other side of the ferry terminal, and picked up the mooring near Goat Island. Once she had her covers on it was time to get into *Worm* and row ashore. It was a lovely calm day, with no wind or swell, so we did not need our lifejackets, but we could not be sure it would the same on the way back in a month, so we had to take them with us anyway. We would not be able to take the compressed gas inflation bottles on the plane though, so took them out.

After stowing *Worm* carefully ashore we walked round towards the bus station. We fly to Glasgow at 12:25 and then take the train home. We'll be back in a month.

Heading South

Flying North
13/07/15

Moored in the bay behind Goat Island

Flying from Stansted to Glasgow, and then to Stornoway is certainly an efficient way of getting north. The Stornoway plane sat on the runway at Glasgow for nearly an hour for some reason, but all that meant was that we only needed to wait 10 minutes for the bus that runs every 2 hours into the centre of Stornoway.

Both Alison and I were glued to the bus window, waiting for our first glimpse of *Robinetta* on her borrowed mooring. The relief when we saw her there, covers still in place, had us grinning at each other. Alison spotted *Worm* too, upturned on the shore near a boat shed where we had left her. Her red anti-fouling looked unusually pink after a month exposed to the air.

We had lunch ashore, then did some shopping before heading round the bay to launch *Worm*. Alison tripped on the way and fell, bruising the palms of both hands quite badly. Not a good start! Putting any pressure on the heel of her hands hurts, but she doesn't think anything is broken.

It seemed like a long walk after that, carrying luggage and shopping, but getting *Worm* across the beach and into the water was easy. It was calm enough not to worry about the lifejackets (we had planned to blow them up with the mouth pieces if it was rough). *Worm*'s oars and floor were safely stowed where we had left them, and she looked none the worse for wear.

We had been warned that sea birds would use *Robinetta* as a perch and they obviously had, but no worse than when we left her a month unattended at West Mersea and I got on with scrubbing the stern and cockpit cover while Alison went below and unpacked.

We had left our damp gloves hanging up in the cabin to air when we left. They were still damp when we returned and were growing a coating of green mould. My hiking boots, left in the hanging locker, were the same, and our pillows were damp too. We would normally have put them in a dry bag, but this time they got left out accidentally. Not a good thing, and Alison realised she had forgotten to pack pillow cases too. Her heart sank at the idea of using T-shirts over the damp pillows: we could do it if we had to, but there was a Tesco just over the water.

We got into *Worm,* and for a change I rowed. We get some comments when I sit relaxed in the stern while Alison rows but the truth is she loves rowing and rarely lets me have a go! I headed for the town side of the bay. There is nowhere to leave a dingy there long term, but there is a broken slipway we could tie her to and walk up. It was high water, so the sewer pipe that runs parallel to the beach was covered. But not enough to let *Worm* float across with two of us in it. Alison had her sea boots on, and got out while I stayed in the boat and floated to land dry shod on the beach.

Alison has had her sea boots for longer than we've had *Robinetta,* but it turns out that she should have replaced them, like I did. This was their first dip in the sea this season, and they both leaked. She walked round Tesco sloshing slightly and wondering why the water didn't run out as quickly as it ran in. Tesco had no pillowcases, but they did have pillows, so we bought a pair. Alison also got some cheap tea towels to sew together into cases, while I picked up some draw string bin bags to stow the new pillows in when we leave. Tesco also supplied a salad, and a hot chicken for our dinner. Bliss!

I phoned Donald MacSween, the generous owner of the mooring, to say thanks, and he replied no problem; it was good to have something keeping the ropes out of the water, so weed and barnacles could not make their homes on it.

We went to bed early, having decided on a 4 am alarm. The winds were forecast to go light tomorrow afternoon, so we want to use the wind while we can.

Gales Every Weekend

A long day's motor

14/07/15

The alarm went at 4 am, but it was 04:50 before we'd drunk our tea and packed the bedding away. We hoisted sail on the mooring and sailed off, with only about 15 seconds of engine assist to get us clear of the buoy and give us steerage way past the moored boats. We were very slow getting clear of Stornoway bay (1½-2 knots) but we sailed anyway.

We laid in a course for Barra, but did not expect to get there. It was a wish that could only come true if the wind stayed west, and it was due to go south west. At sailing speed we would not get there until gone midnight. By 08:00 we knew it would not happen as the wind was on the nose, and we changed our plan, heading south of the Shiants then diagonally across the Minch and down the west coast of Skye. We needed the engine to sail this course too, but at least the wind was helping, until it died away to nothing. The autopilot went on for the first time this year, and by 15:00 we had the main down since it was doing nothing but getting a sun tan.

There were compensations for the motoring. We had blue sky and sea, glorious sunshine and scenery, and the air was warm enough for both us us to lose layers of clothing (honest!) There were small family groups of guillemots sitting on the water, and occasional solitary puffins. Gannets and fulmars flew overhead, but they were rare. Not as rare as yachts though! Alison only spotted 4 all day.

Oisgill Bay, Isle of Skye

When as we passed Loch Pooltiel and had phone signal we phoned Loch Tarbert (Lock Fyne) where we are booked into a traditional boat festival.

Gales Every Weekend

We booked ages ago, when we were first planning our trip, and before we decided to leave *Robinetta* in Stornoway, and have not really looked at the programme. There were no details when we booked, so we wanted to check it was actually going to happen! It is, starting on Friday with a reception, so that is our aiming point, timewise.

There are high winds forecast for the following Sunday so we want to be somewhere sheltered then anyway. We do not have long to get there, but that is okay.

We got the main back up just off Neist Point when we got some wind, but the breeze soon went (the engine was only off for 5 minutes.) There was a bit of swell off the lighthouse; two tide regimes meet here, and for a while we were slowed to 3 knots. We had lost the tide that helped us down the Minch now and progress slowed. We decided to head for an anchorage in Loch Bracadale and stay there for the night. Our ETA showed as 22:00, so we would still have light to anchor.

Neist Point lighthouse, Isle of Skye

By 19:10 we were off An Dubh-sgeir, with a lovely view of the Macleod's Maidens, and about to head into Loch Bracadale, but the next forecast changed out plans. The strong winds were no-longer due on Sunday, but would arrive by Thursday afternoon. When we were planning to go through the Corryvrecken there was a force 7 in the forecast. That is way too much wind to even think of taking *Robinetta* near the place.

With the benign conditions of this evening it made sense to push on as far as possible, to give ourselves more time to take the route through the Sound of Luing on Thursday morning's favourable tide, so we abandoned

Gales Every Weekend

the unexplored beauty of Loch Bracadale, and headed towards Canna. We would not arrive until Midnight, but it is a familiar place, and if we felt up to it we could keep going and do an overnight passage. We raised sail again at 20:00 when the wind came in a little from astern, but there was not much of it, and the boom lifted with every swell, so it only helped a little. We got the sails down again at 22:30 before it became totally dark.

There were a lot of fishing boats gathered on the north shore of Canna, obviously after the same fish as the dolphins that swam past us at 23:00. The dolphins did not stop to play, but it was lovely to see them again. We picked up Canna's pilotage lights, and headed into the harbour on the leading lights. Much easier to see at night than in the daytime!

As we had feared all the moorings were taken, and 3 boats were already anchored, but there was a good gap between the end of the moorings and one of the anchored boats, so we dropped our anchor there. Our anchor light has stopped working, so I hauled an LED lantern up the mast on the spare halyard. Then we turned in at 00:20, with the alarm set for 05:30.

Canna to the Black Isles

15/07/2015

Early morning in Canna Harbour

We didn't want to go down the Sound of Mull again so we looked for a route around the west of Mull. Rubh Ardlanish has an anchorage liked by both Martin Lawrence in the Clyde Cruising Club pilot and by the Antares folks. It is about 50 miles from Canna and 30 from the Dores Mhor so we made it today's 'plan A'. We both woke around 4 but couldn't face getting

Gales Every Weekend

up so we went back to sleep until the 05:30 alarm. I made the tea as usual and we bounced into action. Ok, bounced might be over-stating it.

Coming in so late in calm weather, we had done the bare minimum of putting her to bed. The peak halyard and jib were still in place so we just had to free the halyards from the frapping lines, fit the stay-sail halyard and free the tiller and we were ready to go.

But first breakfast. Stornoway black pudding, fried tomato, bacon and egg.

Then Alison started the engine and I hauled the chain up. The anchor came free really easily with only a little kelp. Anchor stowed, we raised the stay-sail and tensioned the bob-stay and we were off. Hardly any more work than coming off a buoy.

A ketch motored off ahead of us and a sloop raised sail on the mooring and followed us. We left just after 7 and for the second day in a row heard no weather forecast. A mystery we would solve later in the morning.

Once clear of Canna we went head to wind and got the main up. Back on course it was clear that there was enough wind to sail, but not to make 4 knots so we motor sailed.

The route took us around Coll then down the west side of Mull. I wanted to pass east of the Treshnish Isles and down past Staffa but a read of the pilot and the tide tables on the way to Coll told us we would be fighting strong tidal streams that way. So Alison laid in a course outside the Treshnish Isles and Iona.

Eigg and Muck with the Mainland beyond

The weather was stunning, showing off the very best of Rhum, Eigg, Muck and Coll with distant vistas of Ardmamurchan under puffy cumulus clouds with stratos and cirrus above.

We didn't hear the 10:10 weather either. Alison checked the radio and the volume was turned right down. Mystery solved. Alison had tried to turn it off yesterday by turning it down like we did with the old radio and not turned it up again. This morning I had turned it on and assumed the volume was still as I had left it.

We discussed the options for Thursday. The Rubh Ardalanish anchorage left our options open for either the Corryvreckan or the Sound of Luing. It was near springs so the former was only attractive at HW slack which was either too early or too late, while the latter was okay at any favourable tide. The trouble was the favourable tide was 6:45 to noon. That meant a 2 or 3 am start. If the weather stayed fine we should go further on, to an alternative anchorage at Carsaig. Plan B.

We couldn't quite make the course to leave the Dutchman's Cap to port and the gap between it and Lunga looked wide enough that the tide should be weak so we deferred the decision and motor sailed best course to windward as I cooked scotch pies in the Omnia. After lunch it seemed we could nearly make the course and would sail better past Iona if we pinched around the outside. That worked nicely.

Finally at 13:10 we got a weather forecast. It was fine to go on to Carsaig. We would get a night's sleep! Tomorrow's forecast was not too bad either, the high winds we were expecting had slowed, so we did not need to worry about them until Friday.

Just north of Iona the tiller pilot fell off the tiller.

Last year the peg that holds the tiller pilot on the tiller came off on the way from Anstruther to Peterhead. I replaced it with a machine screw and it has lasted until now.

It just sheared off. Alison helmed while I found the packet of machine screws, sawed one to length and fitted it. I cut it as short as possible to minimise the strain.

As we rounded the south-west corner of Mull the wind dropped and the tide kicked in in our favour and we headed east at 5 ½ knots. It got very hot out of the breeze and we peeled layers off including the legs of my Craighoppers. T shirt and shorts at last! 7pm and we had to put sun tan lotion on. We passed the Rubh Ardalanish anchorage almost without noticing it. Carrying on was the right idea. We would be 10 miles closer in the morning.

But Carsaig was horrid. The wind funnelled down the valley and the anchorage was tiny and the wind would blow us towards the rocks. The

Gales Every Weekend

Black Isles were 2 hours away, but promised better shelter and we would be there by midnight. Plan C.

The wind calmed down as soon as we were away from Carsaig and Alison went below for a doze while I helmed. We were crossing a nice deep patch of water with no sign of crab pots, so it was a good idea for one of us to rest and be fresh for anchoring. An hour and a half later it was dark but with fully dark adjusted eyes we could still see as we entered the anchorage. There were already three boats in there, a gaff ketch, a lug schooner and a bermudan sloop. Our gaff cutter added perfectly to the mix!

The thump thump of our single cylinder engine echoed off the sheltering islands, and a light went on one boat, while someone came on deck on another to check us out. The boats were all larger than *Robinetta*, and we easily found enough space in shallower water, well clear of them. The Garmin chart plotter did not have enough detail to be useful but the Navionics charts on my tablet were excellent.

Anchoring was simple and the shelter and holding good. We raised the anchor light and settled down for a quiet night.

Barnabas and Kirsty at the Black Isles

Black Isles to Cairnbaan

16/07/2015

We woke to cloudy skies and after another fine breakfast we raised sail and for the first time in ages we sailed off the anchor. The other yacht crews were up and about too and the bermudan, now identified as a Hallberg-Rassey left just after we did. The folks on the ketch *Kirsty* took our picture as we passed and Alison took theirs.

Reisa Mhic Phaideanin, Sound of Luing

We were so busy enjoying the view that we went the wrong side of Lunga and only noticed because there was no rip. We turned back and crossed into the Sound of Luing and sped down towards the Dorus Mhor.

The skies had cleared into a gorgeous morning as we arrived at Crinan. The lock was full so we picked up a spare mooring and had a cup of tea while we waited for it to cycle through. We locked in with a large bermudan yacht and tied up in Crinan Basin as we wanted some lunch and to visit the chandlers and buy some paint.

Then it was time to leave. We wanted to get to the Ardrishaig basin but we ran out of time getting through the locks, and had to stop for the night at Cairnbaan. It almost felt like we had come home. Our Journey to the West was over.

Gales Every Weekend

Into Loch Fyne

17/07/2015

After a peaceful night at Cairnbaan we headed south along the canal at 09:00, into an obvious headwind. The early forecast was still for SW force 5-7 occasionally 8, but the wind did not feel that strong in the canal. Two large modern yachts locked into the canal basin at Ardrishaig as we prepared to lock out. They reported that it was rough in Loch Gilp, but we decided to give it a go anyway. It is less than 10 miles from Ardishaig to Loch Tarbert, and we were determined to get to the festival!

We got the bowsprit out and the jib bent on in lock no 2, but there was no chance to raise the main and put reefs in it. We got the stay sail up in the sea lock, then motored out at 11:00, letting *Worm* out onto a long line as we went. We think we were the only boat to leave the canal that day.

Leaving Ardrishaig

We were never tempted to unfurl the jib, or raise the main to reef it. Even the stay-sail kept her heeled! We beat down Loch Gilp and into Loch Fyne on stay-sail and engine, keeping up a steady 2-3 knots. The seas were *Robinetta* friendly, in that they did not stop her, but that was due to the fact that we were sailing across them, not straight into them as we would have been just on engine.

We reached East Loch Tarbert at 15:30 after what turned out to be a pleasant time on the water. *Robinetta* rolled a bit, and took the occasional wave over the bow with spray coming aft into the cockpit, but she felt solid and safe. The gusts were fierce, but too short to cause us problems. *Worm* had followed along in her normal problem free fashion, arriving with no water in her at all!

People were waiting to take our lines, others came along to chat and admire *Robinetta*. The Tarbert Traditional Boat Festival is run by very friendly folk.

Tarbert Traditional Boat Festival

19/07/2015

We arrived in Tarbert to a great welcome. Most boats had arrived the day before to avoid the strong winds. There was a grand collection of boats, both local and visitors. The biggest was *Cruinneag III*, a beautiful varnished bermudan cutter ketch built in Tarbert by Dickies in 1936. The smallest was a Drascombe Skaithe. The two boats from farthest afield were *Lassie of Chester*, a Nobby from Bangor and a motor cruiser from Wisbech. At least four boats were from Arran, *Pequita,* a Twister from Lamlash and three boats from Lochranza, a Hillyard 2 1/2 tonner, a Memory 19 and a larger old wooden yacht. Local boats included festival organiser Hans Kok's 1918 gaff ketch *Makkemok*. As well as many sailing vessels there was a good selection of converted fishing boats One must not forget the longship *Freydis* hand built by festival organiser Phil Robertson for his other event, the Viking Festival. Saturday's barbecue was a fund raiser for Phil's aspiration to take her to Norway to participate in festivals there.

Gales Every Weekend

Lassie of Chester

The primary public purpose of the event is to give locals and tourists the opportunity to walk around and look at the boats and talk to the owners. We spent most of Saturday and part of Sunday morning aboard with our hastily scribbled sign showing people around and answering questions.

For the participating crews it was mostly about the craic, but also about sharing skills and knowledge. Douglas, a lad from Loch Ranza had just migrated from dinghies to his first larger boat, a Memory 19 called *Odyssey* which had not been looked after by her previous owner. He had been shown how to sail gaff rig by his friend Robert a self declared 'sea gypsy'. Robert has a Hillyard 2½ tonner called *Storm Petrel*. He bought it as a 'fixer upper', took out the non-working inboard engine and built his own spars, rigging her as a yawl. The sails were from eBay, expertly recut. I helped Douglas set up his bob-stay tension and when the wind died there was a big topsail debate. The general feeling was that it was too big to sheet.

There was a boat moored on our pontoon flying an OGA 50 flag but somehow we never got to meet the folks on board.

We had a reception on Friday evening with good music from local musicians and a fine ceilidh with country dancing and rock covers on Saturday night. It poured with rain and the midges were out in force but we had a grand time.

Saturday afternoon also saw a greasy pole competition and the village raft race. Those able to get out to the end of the greasy pole, grab a bottle and bring it back won a bottle of whisky. The hard part was turning round after getting the bottle, but a few managed it.

Leaving Loch Tarbert

19/07/2015

After a crew breakfast and awards at the Tarbert Hotel the final event of the Traditional Boat Festival was a sail past on Loch Fyne. We motored out of the harbour near the front of a pack of boats, then got our sails up and had a lovely sail with a variety of traditional boats; everything from converted fishing boats to *Cruinneag III*. I took some great pictures.

Kilmory

Some of the boats went back into Tarbert, but many headed straight home.

We sailed across to Portavadie Marina, just across Loch Fyne. We needed diesel after our days of motoring south and Loch Tarbert only has it available Monday to Friday.

Portavadie Marina is too new to be on our chart plotter, and a fish farm confused us slightly but we found the entrance and got the sails down. A fender went overboard while I was tying them on, but we picked it up without problems and headed in. I called them up on the VHS and we got a reply!

We headed straight for the fuel dock and someone was waiting there when we arrived. We had been warned that the fuel was expensive compared to Loch Tarbert, so we just filled the tanks, not the cans, but the whole process was very time effective. It only took half an hour from getting the sails down to raising them again, then we were off on a glorious sail to the Kyles of Bute.

Gales Every Weekend

The scenery was spectacular, and the weather perfect; blue sky, force 3-4 wind, and calm sea, The wind dropped as we approached Kames, so we furled the jib and put the engine on to motor along the shore and look at Tighnabruaich. I spotted some gannets diving, and decided to follow their lead. I had bought new mackerel line at Tarbert and wanted to try it out.

Alison put the engine in neutral and we sailed very slowly (½ knot) along the shore towards Tighnabruich while I let out the mackerel line and trailed it. For the first time ever we caught fish! Two beautiful mackerel took the lure. That that was dinner sorted! Delicious!

Tighnabruaich Pier, Kyles of Bute

The wind came up again, so the engine went off and we sailed up to the Butt of Bute. The wind dropped away again there, so we got the engine on and since it was 1900 and we were close to where we wanted to anchor we got the sails down. We had a look in Caladh Harbour, a very popular anchorage, but it was full as expected, and there was already a yacht in the tiny anchorage by One Tree Island we had been recommended to try. We ended up anchored in 3m of water in the scarily named Wreck Bay. There were already 2 boats there, but there was plenty of room for us.

Wreck Bay to Holy Loch

20/07/2015

Wreck Bay is a very good anchorage, despite the name and provided a perfectly sheltered stop. *Worm* behaved herself too, and we slept in, not stirring until 08:00. Alison blames the Belfast Coastguard! They broadcast the weather report a full hour later than Stornoway, so there is no incentive to be awake at 07:00.

Gales Every Weekend

Lowering clouds had replaced yesterday's sunshine, and our tentative plans to explore the Burnt Isles and the vitrified fort did not survive the weather. We set off at 11:00, motoring through the Burnt Isles then down the Eastern Kyle with very little visibility. We decided to make for Holy Loch, so we could spend the day ashore in Dunoon if the weather got no better tomorrow.

Wreck Bay, Kyles of Bute

It alternately rained and drizzled all day, and the wind was on the bow until we turned up the Firth of Clyde. We got the sails up, and had half an hour of sailing until the wind died away, then the engine went on again. The contrast with yesterday was extreme!

Once tied up in Holy Loch Marina we put the cockpit cover on, and ate dinner on board as there were no restaurants in easy reach. The marina staff had told us there was a pub in the village, so we left *Robinetta* and spent the evening there, using the Internet and soaking up the warmth.

Holy Loch to Kilchattan Bay

22/07/2015

After a day ashore in Dunoon we wanted to get sailing again, so got away from the marina by 09:20. A very broad reach down Holy Loch gave us hope that we would be able to reach down the Clyde, but unfortunately that turned out to be a funnelling effect; when we got into the Clyde we were having to beat. With very little wind, and a fair amount of swell, we put the engine on and motored until the wind got up.

The weather was a bit dreary again, with drizzle and occasional rain, but the rain brought more wind, and by the time we were off Kip we had turned

Gales Every Weekend

the engine off. We furled the jib and reefed during one rain squall, but then got everything up again when our speed dropped to 2 knots. The engine went back on for half an hour, then we needed a reef back in.... It was a day when wind strength varies between F2 and F6, but once in the Clyde the direction was pretty constantly SW. At 13:00 the rain stopped altogether, and the sky had some blue in it.

As we sailed between Great Cumbrae and Bute I spotted rocks off the south end of Bute and asked Alison to look for them on the chart. There were none, and with the aid of binoculars we realised that we could see a surfaced nuclear submarine being escorted north by a number of smaller vessels. Very interesting!

Submarine off Great Cumbrae, with Hunterston beyond

We intended to anchor in Kilchattan bay, but had two contrasting suggestions as to where to drop the hook. The charts put the anchorage on the north side of the bay, off a gently sloping beach. It looked idyllic, but there was a yacht already anchored there that seemed to be rolling a bit. The Clyde Cruising Club directions (2004 edition) give precise instructions for anchoring on the south side, near the houses and between a jetty and a pier. We decided to check it out.

Unlike the north the shore looked rocky, and there was only a small area with the right depth. There was one mooring laid. We motored around for a bit, getting the sails down, and decided the shelter was good enough that it was worth trying to anchor.

We found the right spot and dropped the anchor. It held, so we decided to go ashore for a walk.

The walk from Kilchattan bay to Dunagoil Bay and St Blane's Church then back over the hills to Kilchattan is pretty near perfect. There are standing stones, wonderful views, an atmospheric ruined church, and abandoned farmsteads. Lots to see!

There is wild life too. Alison saw a deer bounding away from us, and we both saw a pair of buzzards (or two) overhead. They were difficult to photograph, but I got a lovely shot of a gold finch. The walk took us two hours, and if we had had another hour we would have detoured to see Dunagoil fort, but as it was we did not get back to *Robinetta* until 21:00.

Dunagoil Fort, Bute

Kilchattan to Arran

23/07/2015

About 04:30 Robinetta started to roll, just like she had in Craighouse last year. By 05:00 it was too bad to sleep, so we put the bed away and by 05:20 we had the anchor up and were motoring out of the bay. Our destination was Arran. I wanted to do a circumnavigation of the island, so we hoped to make Campbeltown, then back up the west side to Loch Ranza tomorrow. Alison suggested that we might want to motor the 3 miles to Great Cumbrae and have breakfast at Millport, but it was a very vague idea and I made a cup of tea instead, I had just hauled up the anchor, and raised the main. We kept the reef in from yesterday.

By the time we were clear of the bay the source of the swell that had woken us was obvious; the sea state in the Clyde was higher than yesterday. The wind was strong too, certainly more than the 4-5 of the forecast. We had not put yesterday's jib away, so I had just hoisted the same one this morning. It was the no.1, too large for today's winds, so I went forward to change it for the no.2. I got soaked as *Robinetta* repeatedly ducked her bowsprit in the water, sending lumps of spray over the foredeck. The drenching was worth it though, as the jib made *Robinetta* much easier on the tiller, but the seas were pretty horrid. Without the engine we slowed to under 3 knots, and the waves stalled her, so we needed the engine on all the time to make progress, as more sail had her heeling too much for safety.

The promised 4-5 SW with slight seas turned out to be 5 gusting 6 with moderate seas. Our next reef down meant dropping the stay sail, which

Gales Every Weekend

meant another soaking trip to the foredeck as the stay-sail never wants to come down even though the halyard can be dropped from the cockpit. Then the stay-sail sheet shackle came off the end of the club foot so I made a third trip forward to secure it.

Meanwhile Alison stayed on the helm and motor sailed our best course to windward. We reefed the main another few rolls as a rain cloud brought stronger winds and steeper seas, then we finally got some protection in the lee of Arran. Conditions were too nasty to want to carry on.

By 10:00 we were in Lamlash Bay, and we picked up a mooring at 10:20. The wind was still fierce but there were no long swells to make to make *Robinetta* roll, so after a cup of tea Alison made porridge, then I cooked bacon rolls. After that we went back to bed. 5 hours of challenging sailing before breakfast is exhausting!

Pequita moored at Lamlash, Arran

Waking at 14:30 we got a second line on the mooring buoy, and made *Robinetta* ship shape, with the jib away and the sail covers on. The wind was still too gusty to want to row ashore, but there was sunshine, so we hung up the oilys and life jackets to dry in the cockpit, and did some maintenance work, then relaxed in the cockpit with a drink and snacks. The wind was dropping, but there were still gusts that would make if unpleasant to row ashore (although fast to row back!)

By 17:00 all the visitor moorings were full, and the moorings boat came by, and took our money.

Then we had another visitor. We had met Luke Furze, who owns the twister *Pequita*, at Tarbert, and he keeps her at Lamlash. We were moored close to his boat, and he saw us there and came over for a chat. After that he very kindly gave us a tow ashore in *Worm* so we could go to the pub for dinner.

Lamlash (Arran) to St Ninian's Bay (Bute)

24/07/2015

We had a very lazy start to the day... With very little wind and bright sunshine we raised the main on the mooring to shake out yesterday's reefs. With the stay-sail and no.1 jib there was just enough wind to sail off the mooring. Then we raised the reaching sail and furled the jib, to make 1-2 knots towards the south end of Holy Isle. We even got the old stay-sail out and rigged a water sail... The main point was to dry the sails, but it made a lovely contract to yesterday's foredeck work!

We lost steerage way after an hour, and were still in Lamlash bay, so the engine went on, and at 3.5 knots instead of ½ we soon reached the red channel marker that marks the end of Holy Isle. Once there we found a little wind, but could only make 2 knots under sail, heading due east. The engine soon went back on, and we headed north, back towards Bute, completing a circumnavigation of Holy Isle instead of Arran!

Holy Isle, Arran

The seas were totally flat so the autopilot went on and we dropped the main sail.

Alison washed the inside of the cabin down with sea water to get rid of the black mould that was creeping back, and I straightened the winch handles and did some fishing (with no catch) while the weather went from warm sun, to light rain, then back again. We had no wind until after lunch, but as soon as we'd eaten the main went up again and we sailed (still on autopilot).

After a lovely gentle sail we dropped anchor in Dunagoil Bay. The water was so clear that we could see the sand 3m below. It was not especially sheltered with the wind now from the NW, so we decided not to spend the night, but we wanted to visit Dunagoil Fort, so Alison rowed ashore while I swam!

Ashore at Dungoil Bay

Watched by curious heifers we moored *Worm* to some rocks and set her anchor in the sand. An easy scramble along the shore brought us to Dunagoil Fort. A lovely place!

We discovered house remains on the summit, plus our first chunk of vitrified fort. We also found fresh puffball mushrooms, and picked enough to add to our dinner.

The row back to *Robinetta* into the swell was not as pleasant as the row to the beach, but Alison managed it with ease, and the anchor came up beautifully clean. We raised sail as we cleared the bay and set off best course to windward.

Robinetta anchored in Dunagoil Bay

We beat north for a couple of hours. The tack towards Arran was depressing, the land being dark and far away, while the sun was in Alison's eyes so she could not easily check the sail set. The swell got up, and she wondered about reefing. She handed me the tiller instead! Then we tacked, and had the sun behind us with Bute to admire. We also sped up, from a slogging 3 knots to 4, and this was the making tack!

We approached St Ninian's Bay, our intended overnight anchorage, and were not sure we had made the right choice. There was one yacht already in there, and it did not look especially sheltered. The Clyde Cruising Club directions said to anchor in 8-9 m, which is deeper than we like. We got the sails down in the bay, and it was calmer than it looked, then as we were motoring towards our chosen anchoring spot another yacht came in under motor and passed us. They were obviously more aware of us than it seemed, and left the area we were aiming for clear.

Once the anchor was dropped and set we realised that the anchorage was great. Despite the cold wind above decks it was peaceful below with no rocking at all.

St Ninian's Bay to Colintraive

25/07/2015

Got up in a very leisurely fashion again, 10:00 before we finished breakfast! However we did have the sail covers off, the jib bent on, and the end of the stay-sail's self tacking track repaired before we ate...

Gales Every Weekend

The knob that stops the stay-sail sheet car sliding off the end of the track had been jury rigged ever since we bought *Robinetta*. Every time we try to put something permanent in place it comes off! We had ignored the current "temporary" set up of gaffer tape, washers and screw for too long, and it needed replacing.

After breakfast I went forward to haul the anchor up. It had held us securely all night, and saw no reason to shift now! We had to motor forward to take the weight off the chain before I could move it, but it came up clean. We tried sailing once we were out of the bay but progress was too slow even after we tried the reaching sail, and changed up to the no. 1 jib, so the engine went back on and we headed up the West Kyle towards Tighnabruaich.

Waverley at Tighnabruaich pier

Once there we anchored and had lunch, then rowed ashore in search of ice cream. Tighnabruaich was bustling! The paddle steamer *Waverley* was moored up at the pier, the life boat station had an open day and a raft race had just finished. The weather was glorious too; bright warm sunshine!

We made the most of the day!

Once back on *Robinetta* I decided that my trousers were too filthy to wear to the pub we were heading for. Due to a packing error I only had one pair with me, so I got back into *Worm* and washed them over the side. Alison gave me some 'Ecover' washing up liquid, rather than laundry detergent. They are "solar dry" Craighoppers, so there was every chance they would be dry by the time we reached our destination!

Doing the laundry at Tighnabruaich

We raised the main and sailed off the anchor without turning the engine on, which is not something we do often! There was twice the anchor's weight in kelp hanging off it when I hauled it up! The old fashioned fisherman's anchor has really worked well for us this trip. It is the only anchor that can deal with kelp, and it's not been a problem in sand or rock either.

We sailed in fluky winds to and through the Burnt Isles to Colintraive, on the edge of gybing several times, but never actually doing it. The Clyde Cruising Club directions says how variable the winds can be here, and they went from a fine reach to a dead run with hardly a moment's notice. As the wind speed varied between force 1-3 it was interesting and fun, rather than hard work.

We got the sails down at Colintraive, ready to pick up a mooring, but left the staysail up as we often do. This was a mistake here, as it kept blowing *Robinetta's* head round making us look like amateurs, but once we dropped the sail steering became simple and we picked up the buoy without any other problems.

We looked at the weather in the pub that evening, and decided on an early start. Tomorrow afternoon promised F6 gusting 7-8, with rain. It would be good to be safely in Holy Loch Marina before then.

Gales Every Weekend

Colintraive to Holy Loch

26/07/2015

Passage past the Burnt Isles, Kyles of Bute

We came off the mooring at 06:55, and motored down the East Kyle, with what little wind there was ahead of us. It was a grey morning, but dry, with good visibility, and within the hour we had the sails up and were on a close reach past Port Bannatyne. After that the trip just got better! The sky brightened and showed us some blue, and we had a lovely sail up the Cowal coast, only having to tack once as we rounded Towards Head. We started with full main, and ended up with it as reefed as it can get, but we carried the number 2 jib and staysail the whole way.

By the time we reached Holy Loch the sky had clouded over, and the seas were getting up, but we had timed it pretty perfectly. Going head to wind we shook the reef out before towering the main, then motored into the marina and onto the fuel dock. The only thing wrong with today's sail was the temperature. Alison looks forward to sailing when not wearing full oilskins on top of four layers!

We are going to be getting *Robinetta* out of the water for the winter at Fairlie Marine, and putting her in their shed for some TLC. That will happen sometime in October, but we have no firm plans to sail her again before that (although we hope for some time in September) That means we need somewhere to keep her until then.

Alison investigated possibilities, and leaving her at Holy Loch Marina turned out to be the best. They offered us their summer mooring rate, rather than a monthly visitor rate, and she will be safer in a marina with someone keeping an eye on her than on a mooring.

Next morning we moved *Robinetta* from the visitor's area to a berth much closer to the marina office, and put her covers on. *Worm* is ashore and upside down to keep her dry. Leaving them both with an 'end of the season' feeling in July feels sad, but we have had nearly six weeks on board already this season, and I don't have much holiday left!

Last Sail of the Season

Back on board

25/09/2015

Back on *Robinetta* after nearly 9 weeks away!

We got up early to drive up to Scotland, and left Bishop's Stortford at 05:15. Being so early meant we avoided all the traffic hold-ups, and we reached Fairlie Quay at 12:45 after a very pleasant drive. We left the car there, and took to the buses, which got us to the ferry terminal at Gourock. Then it was onto the ferry to Hunters Quay, and a walk along Holy Loch to Sandbanks, and we were on board *Robinetta* by 15:15.

We had been wondering about having an afternoon sail, but getting *Robinetta*'s covers off, and the mould washed off the eating and cooking utensils left us with no energy after our early start. The mould was not nearly as bad as when we got on her at Stornoway; putting things into rubbish bags and sealing them up was a very useful exercise.

We went to the local shop and bought the makings of a cooked breakfast, plus milk for tea, then headed the Holy Loch Inn for an early dinner.

Holy Loch to Largs via Loch Long

26/09/2015

top of Holy Loch

Invited Robert Hill to join us for breakfast as he has his boat *Sagen* at Holy Loch, and drove up yesterday to get her ready to come out of the water. A lovely start to the day! Weather was grey, and very still. There were wreaths of cloud hanging on the hills, going nowhere. We had hoped to go for a sail, but there was too little wind to use, so after we launched *Worm* we just set off under motor to explore a little way up Loch Long.

We skirted the exclusion zone around the submarine base, and passed the entrance to Loch Goil, then carried on as far as Portincaple before turning back down towards the Clyde and Fairlie where *Robinetta* is booked to be hauled out on Sunday morning.

Portencaple shoreline

The wind got up a little as we passed Dunoon, so we got the sail up and turned the engine off near the Gantock Cardinal. Unfortunately we were sailing at less than 2 knots even with the tide in our favour, so after a quiet cup of tea the engine went back on again.

The sun burnt through the overcast around 16:00, and the wind increased again so the sails went back up again and we turned the engine off. The wind direction had us sailing towards the wrong side of Great Cumbrae, so after a pleasant half hour of gentle sailing the engine went back on as we headed to Large Yacht Haven to tie up just before 19:00.

Largs to Fairlie

27/09/ 2015

It would be difficult for Fairlie Quay Marine to be closer to Largs Yacht Haven! A mere ten minutes motoring would see *Robinetta* at her final destination of the year, so we walked to Fairlie last night and collected our car. This morning Alison packed up the cabin and began to transport its contents to the car while I took off the main sail in bright sunshine.

We used the lovely clean and dry pontoons at Largs to properly flake the main and jibs before bagging them up, and two trolley loads later there was very little left aboard. It was much easier to do this than pass everything down while *Robinetta* is up on a cradle!

Approaches to the pontoon at Fairlie are tide dependant; I helmed and reported that there were only 2 metres under the keel across the bay but that is plenty! Alison phoned the office to say we were on our way and there were two people waiting to take our lines then check *Robinetta*'s hull shape and lift points. We hauled *Worm* onto the pontoon, and Alison put the kettle on for a cup of tea.

After a short wait while they set up the hoist we motored under it and the lift began.

On board for the lift out at Fairlie

I've never been aboard during a lift out before. It is a strange experience to see the sides of the dock coming down to meet us! When *Robinetta*'s bow was level with the dock we were told to step over the bow and disembark, so did so.

Robinetta did not get power washed last Autumn. Paul Drake had told us to avoid it for a couple of seasons while the putty hardened up, so Alex and Alison scrubbed her down by hand which had taken a while despite her being quite clean to begin with. I wondered if we should do the same this year and we discussed it with the yard men while the lift out finished. Once she was out we just looked at her. The only obviously fouling was a little weed on the water line, and a few barnacles right at the bottom of the keel (which is impossible to anti foul) and by the propeller.

One of the yard staff scraped off the barnacles, then he power washed around the water-line to remove the weed. The rest of the hull only needed a rinse! We got asked what anti-foul we used, and congratulated on our choice. Tiger Extra seems to work well in the clear Scottish water, although

Gales Every Weekend

mid-season scrubs are vital in the muddy Essex creeks.

Once *Robinetta* was clean the hoist carried her over to the cradle, while we went back to the pontoon to collect *Worm*. At this point Alison remembered that she had left the kettle heating on the stove on aboard *Robinetta*....

Ashore at Fairlie

The yard staff quickly dug out a ladder, and Alison climbed aboard as soon as *Robinetta* was in the cradle. The water was boiling gently, and no harm was done!

Robinetta will be going into the shed next week, which means the mast needs to come out. I pulled the VHF antenna cable on-deck and undid all the halyards from the horse and tied all the free ends around the mast, leaving only the shrouds and fore-stay for the yard to deal with. Hopefully the lines can stay on the mast this winter. I always get things wrong dressing it in spring. *Worm* will stay with *Robinetta* for a change, taking advantage of the shed storage too.

We moved the last few things out of the cabin and into the car, then headed home. Our 2015 sailing season was over.

In the Shed

1/11/2015

Half term means heading north to Largs and getting started on the winter work. *Robinetta* is under cover for the first time since we've owned her, and Alison says that it is nice to know that when she mops out the bilges they are not going to fill again until *Robinetta* comes out of the shed!

She had a good look at the bulwarks where I found some rot at the start of the season. Luckily it is not as bad as it could have been, and she scraped out the really soft bits and in the hope that the rest will dry out before February when I will rout out the rot and insert a new bit of Siberian larch.

Alex spent all week painting the hull. It took that long because there were places that were down to bare wood, which needed two coats of grey metallic primer then two coats of undercoat before the toplac went on, then a final coat of Toplac on all over. In the pauses waiting for the paint to dry he sanded down the gaff, boom, and bowsprit, plus most of the varnished wood on the hull and rudder, and gave them three coats of varnish. Robinetta's paint work is still not finished though, since the bulwarks will need painting in the spring.

The portholes in the forward bulkhead have started to leak when it rains, so we've taken them out to let the wood around them dry out thoroughly, then we'll put them back with new mastic. There are also a couple of persistent leaks just under this bulkhead that needs tracking down.

We need the hatch surrounds rebuilt since they've been leaking for the last couple of years, but I don't feel confident in my woodworking skills and do not have time, so we will be getting those done professionally. Meanwhile Alison will remake the galley again, to accommodate the Orego stove. We've used it successfully for two seasons now, but I would like to get it on gimbals if I can.

Alison also spent a fair amount of time grubbing around in the engine area during the week, cleaning it up and giving regular doses of WD40 to the thru-hulls for the cockpit self drainers. These have been open ever since we bought *Robinetta*, and we never even thought about them since we were told they did not work. The surveyor who looked at *Robinetta* last winter reported that they were open, and the pipes that led upwards from the hull fitting were brittle and needed replacing. We replaced the pipes before launch, but could not get the thru-hulls to close, so we blocked them off at the top instead. I asked one of the boat builders about sealing the openings in the hull, and he said it would be much better to make them movable! He advised the WD40, and after three days of twice daily applications there was finally some movement. By the end of the week, when I could finally join Alex and Alison at the boat shed, the WD40 had worked through enough that I could get the cones out of the holes. I brought them home to clean, and will repair the linkages to the remote opening handles before I return them in February.

Season Totals

We had two distinct cruises this year. The first took us up to Stornoway, in three weeks, while the second brought us back south to cruise inside the Clyde. These were bookmarked by delivery trips, one from last winter's storage at Cairnbaan, and one to this winter storage at Fairlie Quay.

Year totals

Engine-hours	127.75
passage-hours	216
distance	693.5
days-under-way	28
nights on boards	42

Maintenance days 23 (split between 3 people)

The time we spend on maintenance varies each year. This year we did the work in blocks, with three of us working on her in the Spring and Autumn. Alison did a little painting before we left her on the mooring in Stornoway, but did not touch *Robinetta* again until she went into the shed. This made it feel as though we got a lot of sailing compared to maintenance time and with the work Alex did in October it feels as though most of the painting and varnishing for next season has been done already! There is still a lot to do to get *Robinetta* ready for next season, but that is for next year, when we return to Largs in February.

Gales Every Weekend

Place	Arrival Date	No of nights	Type
Cairnbaan	14-4-15	1	Pontoon
Crinan	15-4-15	1	Quayside
Tobermory	16-4-15	1	Pontoon
Tobermory	17-4-15	5 weeks	Mooring buoy
Isle Ornsay	25-5-15	1	Mooring buoy
Plockton	26-5-15	3	Mooring buoy
Loch Hourn	29-5-15	1	Anchorage
Mallaig	30-5-15	3	Marina Pontoon
Inverie	2-6-15	1	Mooring buoy
Canna	3-6-15	1	Mooring buoy
Eriskay	4-6-15	1	Mooring buoy
Lochboisdale	5-6-15	2	Marina pontoon
Loch Maddy	7-6-15	1	Pontoon
Plocrapool	8-6-15	1	Anchorage
Loch Shell	9-6-15	1	Anchorage
Stornoway	10-6-15	3	Marina pontoon
Stornoway	13-6-15 to 13-7-15	30	Mooring buoy
Canna	14-7-15	1	Anchorage
Black Islands	15-7-15	1	Anchorage
Cairnbaan	16-7-15	1	Pontoon
East Loch Tarbert	17-7-15	2	Marina pontoon
Wreck Bay	19-7-15	1	Anchorage
Holy Loch Marina	20-7-15	2	Marina pontoon

Gales Every Weekend

Kilchattan Bay	22-7-15		1	Anchorage
Lamlach Bay	23-7-15		1	Mooring buoy
St Ninian's Bay	24-7-15		1	Anchorage
Colintraive	25-7-15		1	Mooring buoy
Holy Loch Marina	26-7-15 to 25-9-15		9 weeks	Marina pontoon
Largs Yacht Haven	26-9-15		1	Marina pontoon
Fairlie Quay	27-9-15		6 months	Inside Storage

Printed in Dunstable, United Kingdom

67283831R00049